MAORI ARTS OF THE GODS

DEIDRE BROWN

PHOTOGRAPHY BY
BRIAN BRAKE

RAUPO

A RAUPO BOOK
Published by the Penguin Group
Penguin Group (NZ), 67 Apollo Drive, Rosedale,
North Shore 0632, New Zealand (a division of Pearson New Zealand Ltd)
Penguin Group (USA) Inc., 375 Hudson Street,
New York, New York 10014, USA
Penguin Group (Canada), 90 Eglinton Avenue East, Suite 700, Toronto,
Ontario, M4P 2Y3, Canada (a division of Pearson Penguin Canada Inc.)
Penguin Books Ltd, 80 Strand, London, WC2R 0RL, England
Penguin Ireland, 25 St Stephen's Green,
Dublin 2, Ireland (a division of Penguin Books Ltd)
Penguin Group (Australia), 250 Camberwell Road, Camberwell,
Victoria 3124, Australia (a division of Pearson Australia Group Pty Ltd)
Penguin Books India Pvt Ltd, 11, Community Centre,
Panchsheel Park, New Delhi – 110 017, India
Penguin Books (South Africa) (Pty) Ltd, 24 Sturdee Avenue,
Rosebank, Johannesburg 2196, South Africa

Penguin Books Ltd, Registered Offices: 80 Strand, London, WC2R 0RL, England

Originally published by Reed Publishing (NZ) Ltd, 2005

First published by Penguin Group (NZ), 2008
1 3 5 7 9 10 8 6 4 2

Design by Sally Fullam
Printed in by Everbest Printing Co. Ltd, China

ISBN: 978 0 14 301027 2

A catalogue record for this book is available
from the National Library of New Zealand.

www.penguin.co.nz

CONTENTS

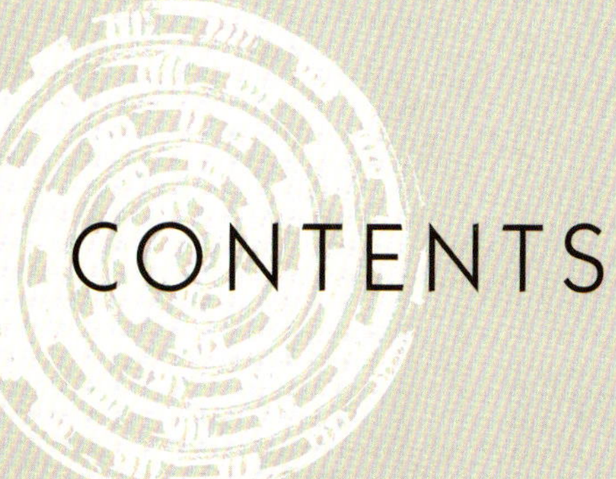

ACKNOWLEDGEMENTS 4

INTRODUCTION 5

1. RANGINUI & PAPATUANUKU 6

2. TANE 14

3. TANGAROA 30

4. TUMATAUENGA 46

5. RONGOMATANE 52

6. HINENUITEPO & HINETITAMA 60

7. MATAORA 72

8. NIWAREKA 78

9. RAUKATAURI 84

GLOSSARY 92

SELECT BIBLIOGRAPHY 94

ACKNOWLEDGEMENTS

Maori Arts of the Gods uses widely accepted interpretations of Maori narratives to recount the origins, concepts and purpose of customary arts. The stories are drawn from Ross Calman's comprehensive revision of A.W. Reed's *Reed Book of Maori Mythology* (2004), and it is acknowledged that in some tribal regions these stories may be retold differently. Further reading material was generously provided by Ross Collinson from his family library. The arts themselves are illustrated with photographs taken by the late Brian Brake, most of which were previously published in *Maori Art: The photography of Brian Brake* (2003). They are beautiful images that demonstrate Maori artistry in a way that words could never explain. These photographs are received with sincere gratitude to the Brian Brake Estate. All the taonga, or treasures, pictured have their own stories, which readers may want to pursue further, and every care has been taken to identify them although, inevitably, there may be some errors of interpretation. The assistance of the following people in clarifying the accession details is acknowledged: Des Cotman (Far North Regional Museum); Roger Neich and Chanel Clarke (Auckland Museum Tamaki Paenga Hira); Daniel McKnight (Hawke's Bay Cultural Trust); Anna Marie-White (Puke Ariki); Michelle Horwood (Whanganui Regional Museum); Awhina Tamarapa (Museum of New Zealand Te Papa Tongarewa); Roger Fyfe (Canterbury Museum); Moira White (Otago Museum); and Leslie Jessop (Hancock Museum, Newcastle-on-Tyne). The production of this book was an initiative of Reed Publishing.

INTRODUCTION

Maori narratives about the gods recount the creation of the world, the arrangement and relationships between its physical parts, the origin and use of all plant and animal species, and the importance of spirituality as a guide for living. They also describe the development, meaning and function of art. Maori customary arts have their foundation in the stories of the gods. In the creation story of the separation of Ranginui and Papatuanuku, as light poured into the world, the first colours experienced were black, white and red — and these have become 'traditional' pigments used in carving, fibre work, and other arts. The conflict between the departmental gods after creation, and their interactions with the natural world around them, led to the arts of wood carving, plaiting, weapon-making and body adornment. Descendants of these gods further developed the arts, including music and musical instruments. The mortal world had a physical relationship to Rarohenga, the underworld, and later characters moved between the realms, creating containers that embodied the journey between life and death, as well as acquiring skills in ta moko, or Maori tattooing, and fibre arts that they were able to bring to the mortal world before the passageway to Rarohenga was finally closed.

1. RANGINUI & PAPATUANUKU

The story of Maori art has its origins in the Creation narrative, which recounts the separation of the primeval parents Ranginui and Papatuanuku. Indeed, skilled kaikorero (Maori orators) can use the narrative to explain the origin of every element of the indigenous world. The parents' offspring originally dwelt in the crevices and folds of a dark universe formed by Ranginui and Papatuanuku's close and perpetual embrace. Eventually, some of the siblings resolved to end their confinement and separate the parents by pushing them apart; the chaos that ensued is illustrated as openwork spirals in many pare (door lintel; pl. 1A & 1B), taurapa (war canoe stern; pls 3L & 3M) and tauihu (war canoe prow; pl. 3I) wood carvings. As the couple were separated, Te Po, the black dark, was broken by Te Ao, the white light, the violence of the separation causing injury and whero (red) blood to flow (pl. 1C). In this way, three fundamental colours of Maori art — black, white and red — were created. Ranginui was pushed upward, where he became the sky father, while Papatuanuku remained as the earth mother. Not all of their offspring were contented with the separation, and the first artistic productions — weapons and traps — were manufactured as they sought vengeance by attacking each other's domains. Tangaroa, and sometimes the god of war Tumatauenga, are both described as plaiting nets and snares to catch the children of Tane, the forest god, and Tane is credited with carving canoes and spears to hunt the progeny of Tangaroa, the sea god. The retelling of these narratives explains the origin of kowhaiwhai (painting), raranga (plaiting), and whakairo rakau (wood carving) and, as practices from the Creation period, expresses their significance as arts of the gods.

The realm occupied by Maori gods and other supernatural beings is often referred to as Hawaiki, sometimes described as a geographical place of origin, but always as a spiritual homeland for supernatural beings, the unborn and spirits of the dead. All customary Maori art could be claimed to be set in Hawaiki, as mythological and ancestral figures appear to be situated in a locationless timeless place, without any depiction of landscape or period, more akin to a memory of a homeland or a Pacific heaven. Migration traditions often refer to Hawaiki as the embarkation point for voyages to Aotearoa New Zealand, and these stories can be related to the great journeys of discovery and settlement that people from the western Pacific made across Oceania over several thousand years. Maori ancestors are thought to have come from central Polynesia between 800 and 1000 years ago, and traces of this artistic heritage can be seen in art from the early settlement period, such as the Kaitaia carving (pl. 1D) which displays the simple humanoid features, edge notching and chevron patterns found in Polynesian art.

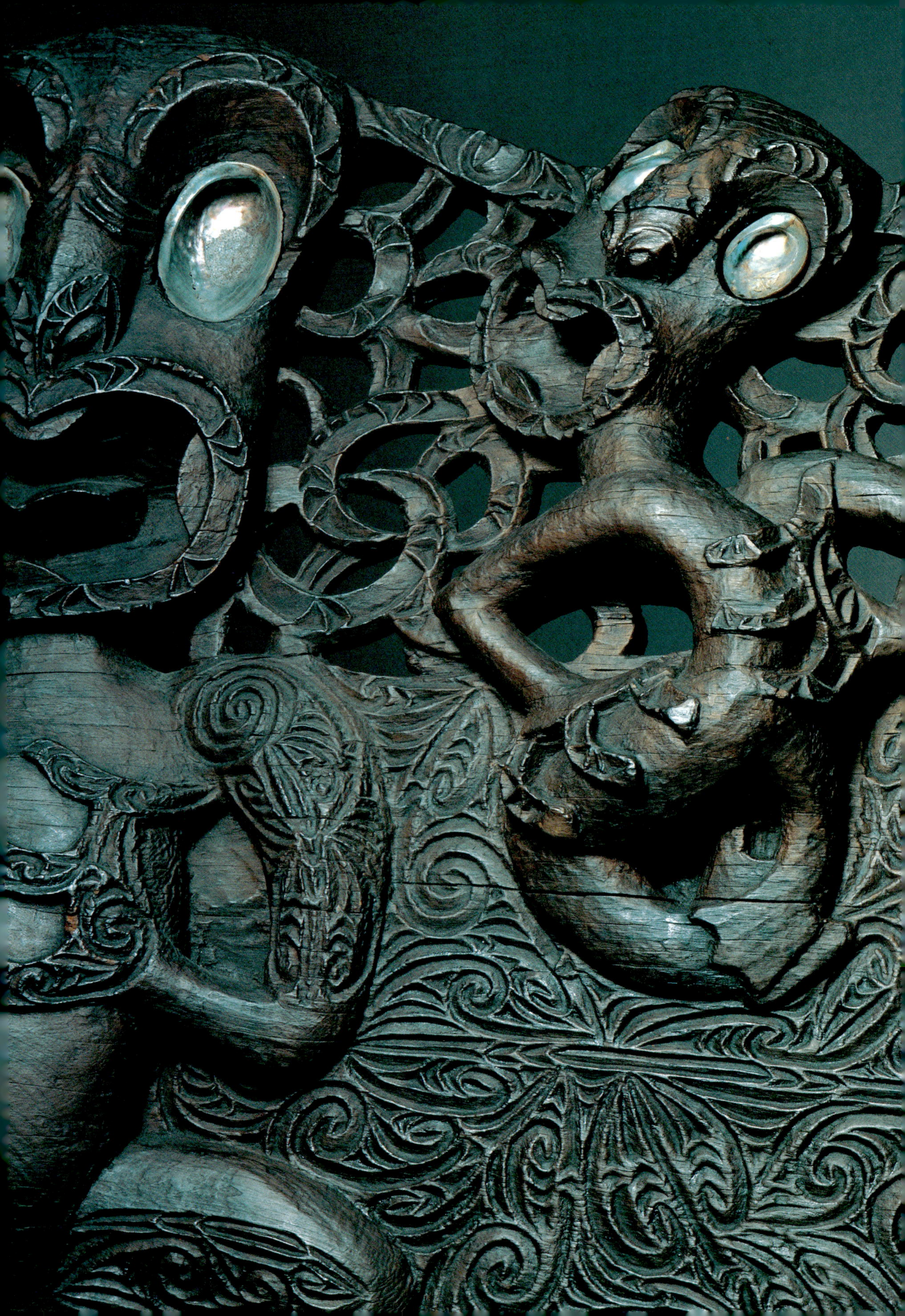

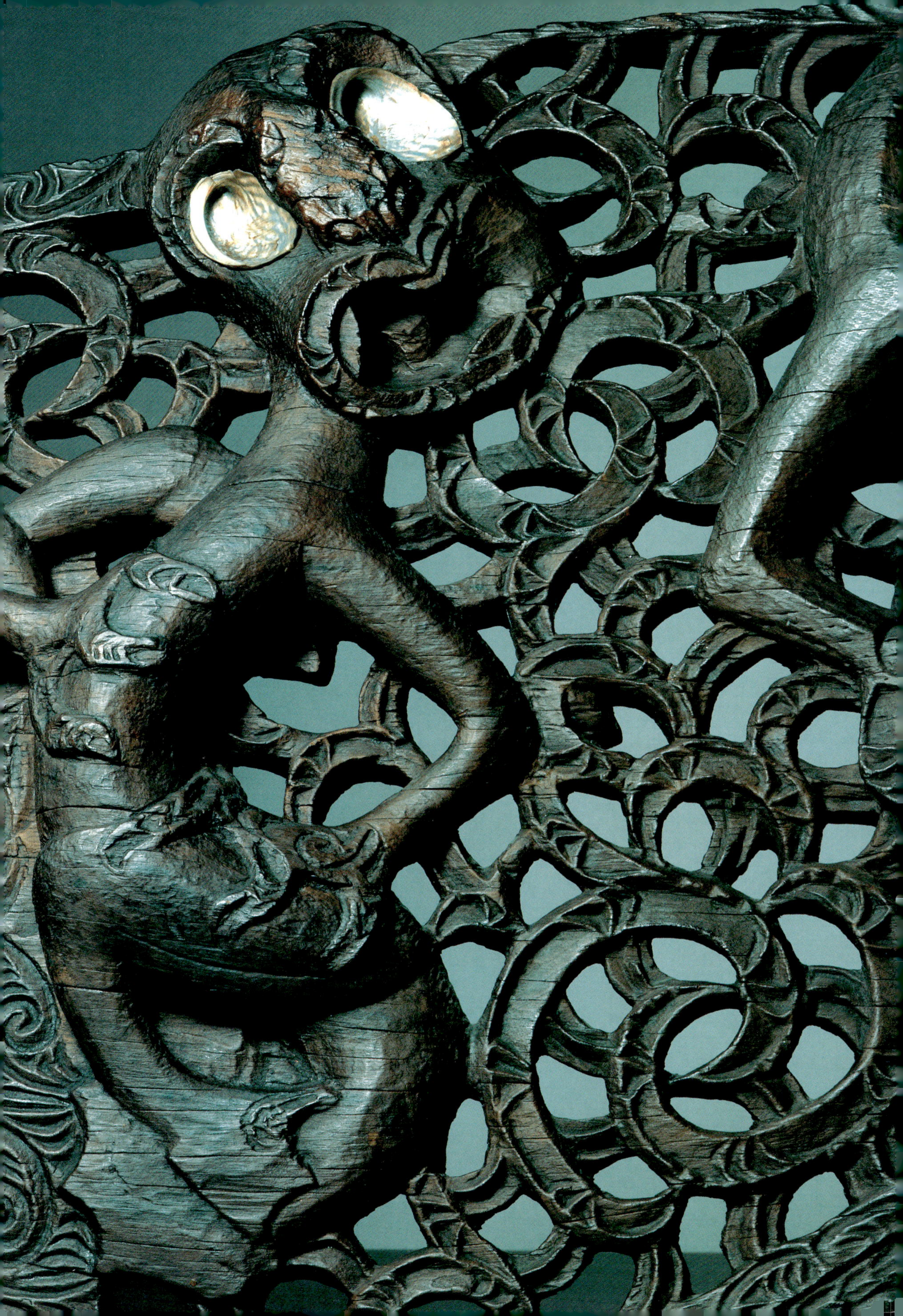

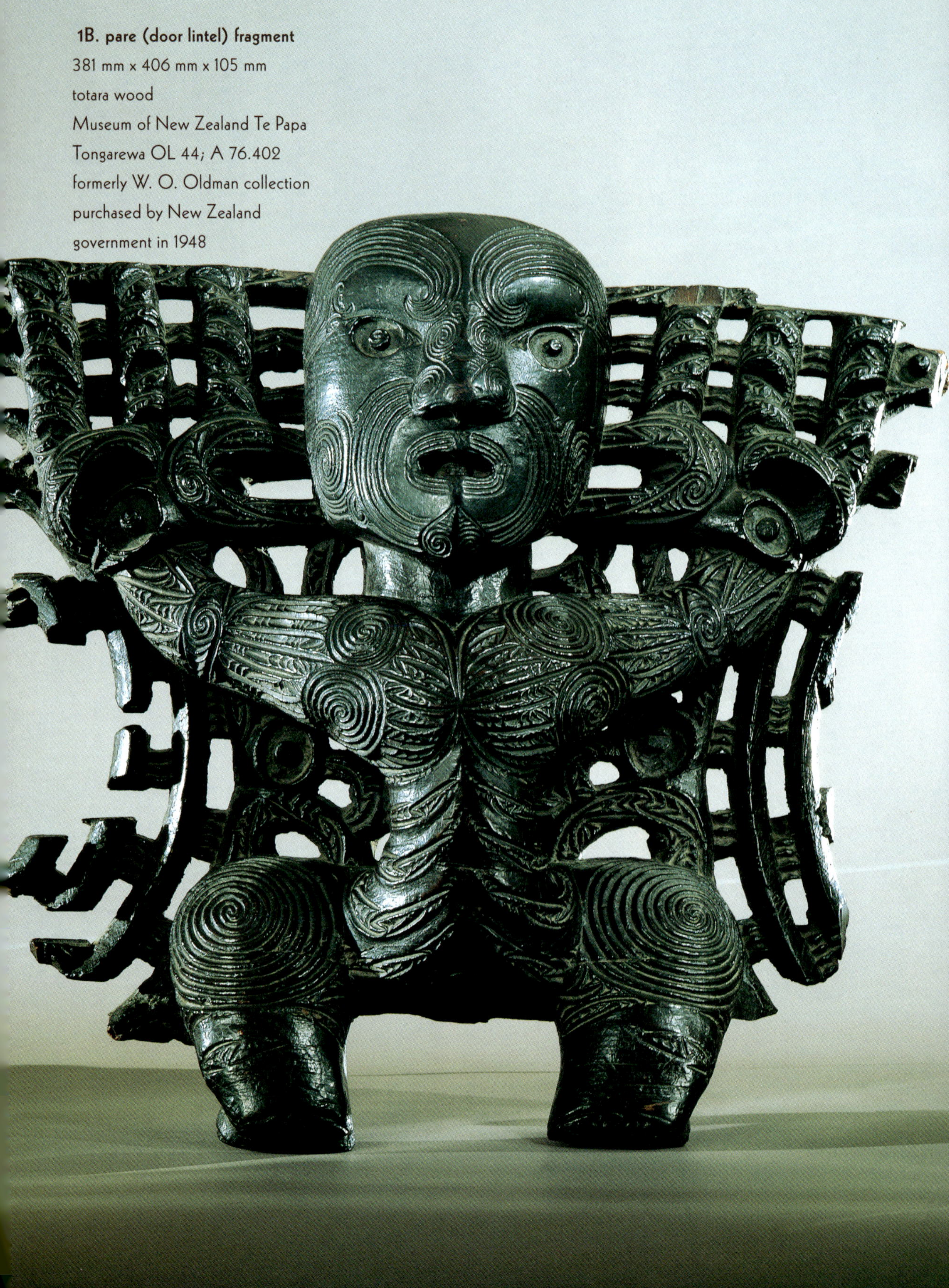

1B. pare (door lintel) fragment
381 mm x 406 mm x 105 mm
totara wood
Museum of New Zealand Te Papa
Tongarewa OL 44; A 76.402
formerly W. O. Oldman collection
purchased by New Zealand
government in 1948

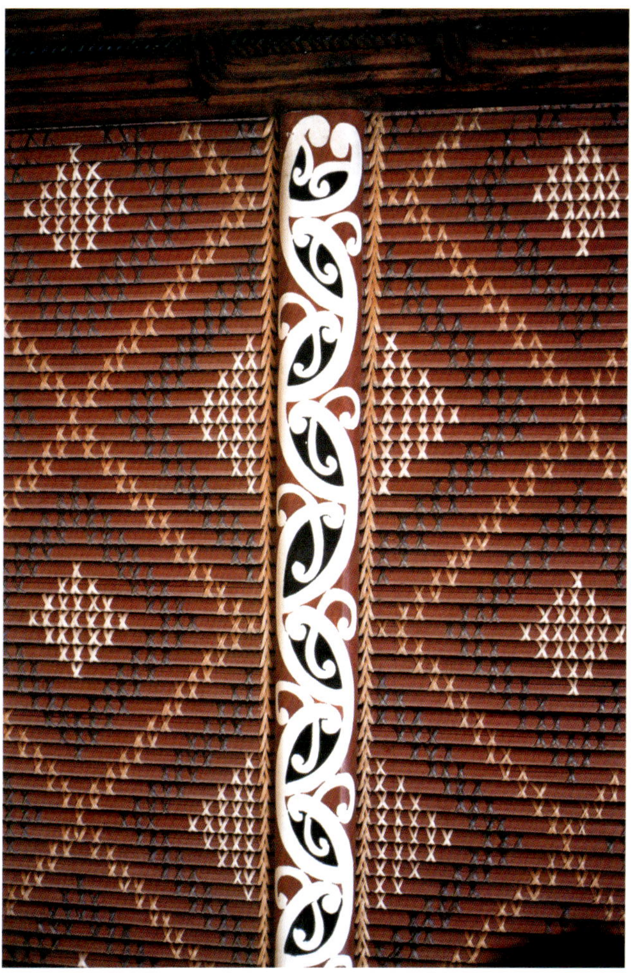

^ 1C. **kowhaiwhai (red, white and black scroll painting) and tukutuku (lattice wall panels)**
attributed to Rongopai meeting house
built at Waituhi in 1887 by Ringatu adherents

« 1A. **pare (door lintel)**
2.350 m (l) x 840 mm (h) x 400 mm (w)
wood, shell
found in a drain at Patetonga, Hauraki
Auckland Museum Tamaki Paenga Hira AM 6189
formerly Leonard Carter collection, purchased by the
museum in 1918

1D 'Kaitaia Carving', whakairo rakau

(carving; possibly for a gateway)

2.25 m (l) x 220 mm (h)

totara wood

found in a swamp at Pukepoto

(between Ahipara and Kaitaia)

Auckland Museum Tamaki Paenga Hira AM 6341

purchased from J. J. Clarke, 1921

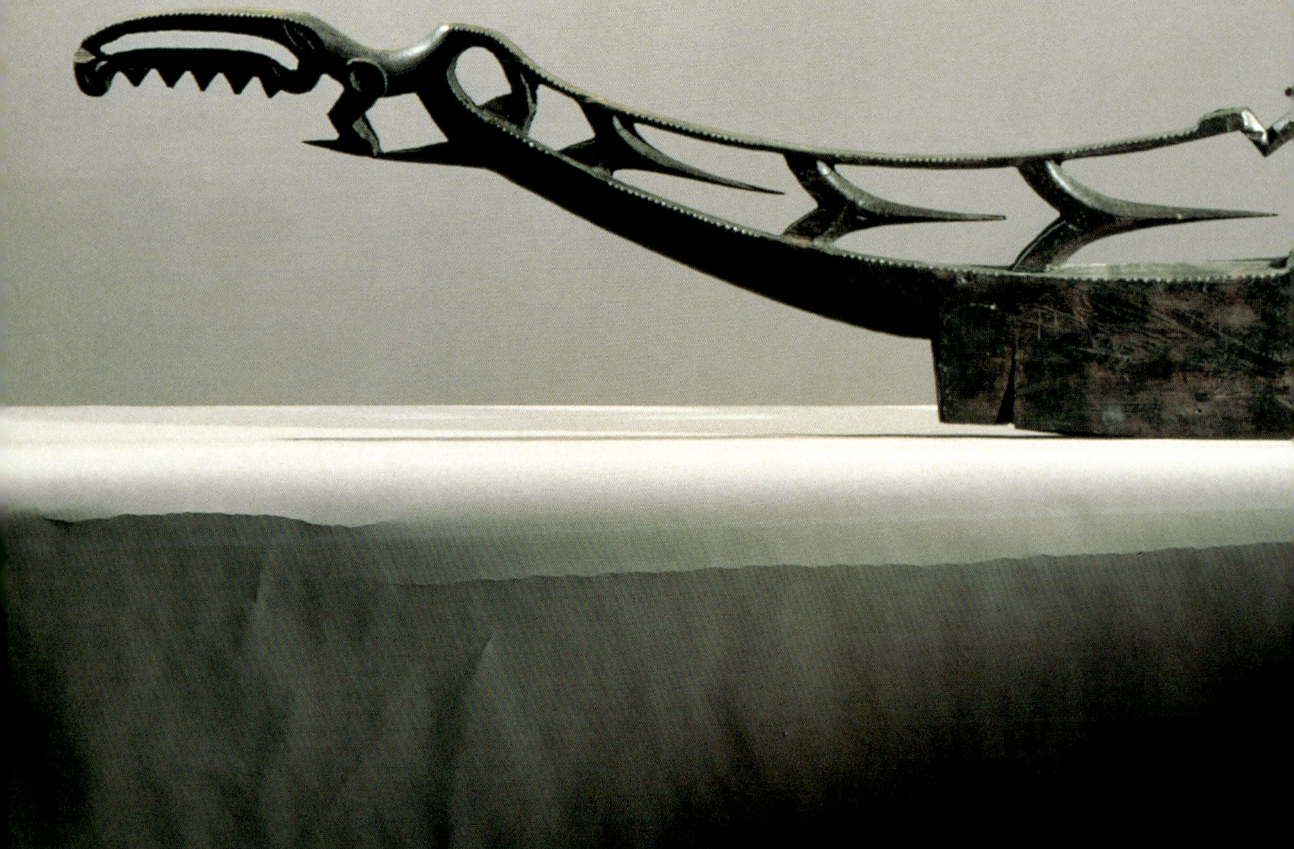

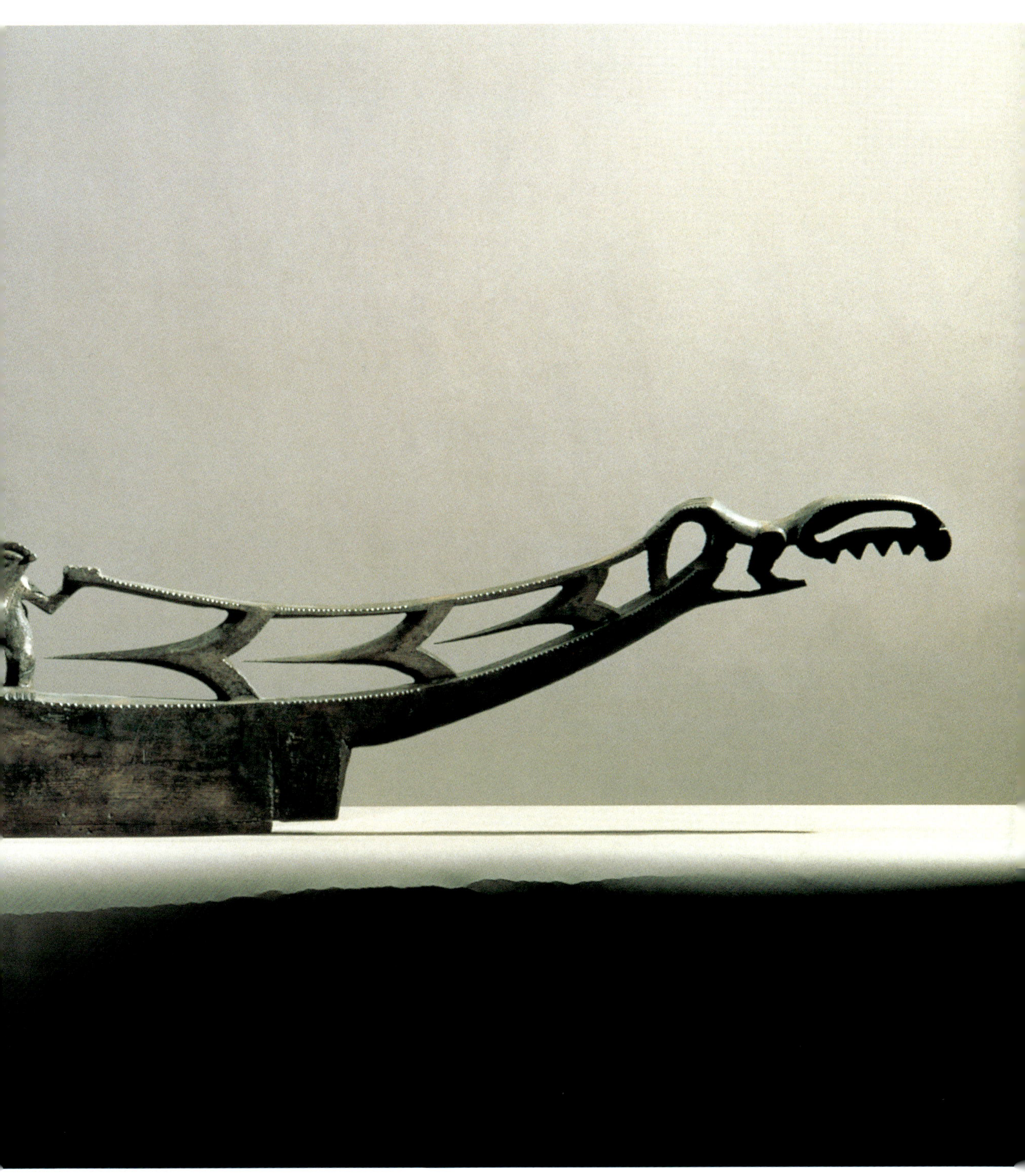

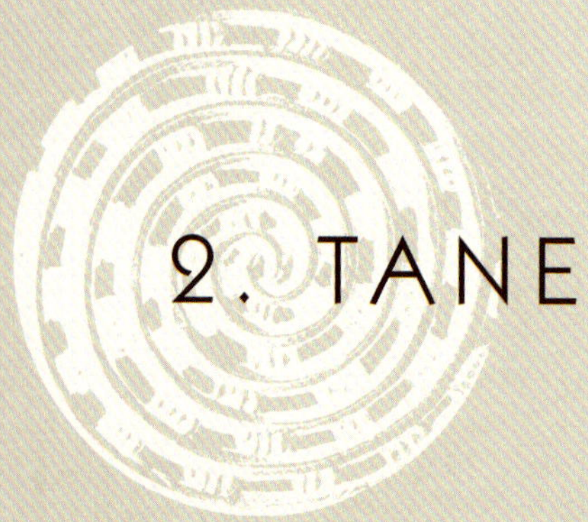

2. TANE

Tane is the most important of the departmental gods, the children of Ranginui and Papatuanuku, as his roles include the separator of the primeval parents, the progenitor of people and land-based natural life, and the provider of knowledge. As god of the forest, he is an important character in the story of wood carving. He is the god invoked, consulted and thanked in karakia (incantations) before trees are felled, the timber regarded as having the mauri (life force) and wairua (everlasting spirit) of Tane even after it is cut and fashioned into other taonga (treasures). He is also the provider of plant fibre used to make tukutuku (lattice wall panels; pls 2A & 2B), sails, mats, baskets and garments.

Today the most significant taonga associated with Tane is the wharenui (meeting house) as it is the largest and most complex art work made from his elements (pl. 2B). A whare whakairo (decorated meeting house) is regarded as the body of an ancestor, a representation of whakapapa (geneaology), and a microcosm of the local world view. Outside the building, the koruru (front gable apex mask) is the head of the ancestor, the maihi (bargeboards) the arms, and the kuwaha (door) the mouth, and inside the tahuhu (ridgepole) the backbone, and the heke (rafters) the ribs. If the house is conceived of as a whakapapa then the tekoteko (front gable apex figure) is the founding ancestor and the descent line runs along the tahuhu, then through the kowhaiwhai painted heke, and down to the more recent ancestors carved on poupou (wall posts). Kaikorero can create narratives about the local world view from the whare whakairo by referring to people and related events depicted in its architectural arts.

The whare whakairo developed during the mid nineteenth century in the central and eastern North Island as an amalgam of the carved pataka (raised storehouse; pls 2C & 2D) and chief's house, proportioned to the same scale as mission churches. The oldest extant carved meeting house is Te Hau-ki-Turanga, built in Turanga (also known today as Gisborne) in the early 1840s by the celebrated Rongowhakaata tribal leader and tohunga whakairo (master carver) Raharuhi Rukupo. A carved figure (pl. 2E) just inside the door is thought to be Rukupo or his late brother Tamati Waka Nene, for whom the house may have been a memorial. Whichever he is, this man is someone of great mana (prestige, status), a quality recognised in his moko kanohi (facial tattoo) and the toki poutangata (ceremonial adze) he holds. Such toki (pl. 2F) were not made to be used to carve wood, but to signify the owner's importance as a leader and cultural expert.

Over time regional figurative carving styles and systems of architectural embellishment have developed. A general style division exists in the North Island, between the northern and western regions, where carvings depict sinuous-bodied figures (pl. 2K), and the central and eastern districts, where the bodies are square and upright (pl. 2H). Artists in some eastern regions would highlight parts of carvings with multicoloured pigments (pls 2I & 2J), as distinct from other methods of monochromatic pigmentation using red ochre (pl. 2G) or black swamp deposits. With the appropriation of Western methods of portraiture, and European pigments, naturalistic figurative painting became popular and for some groups, most notably late nineteenth century Ringatu Church followers, it replaced carved and woven architectural embellishments, as can be seen in the Rongopai meeting house (pl. 2L), built at Waituhi in 1887. Customary methods of design were eventually revived in the late 1920s and 1930s, and in more recent times polychromatic art and new approaches to carving using laminated particle board sheets (pl. 2M), pioneered by Paratene Matchitt and Cliff Whiting, have continued innovations in Maori architecture and, ultimately, the arts of Tane.

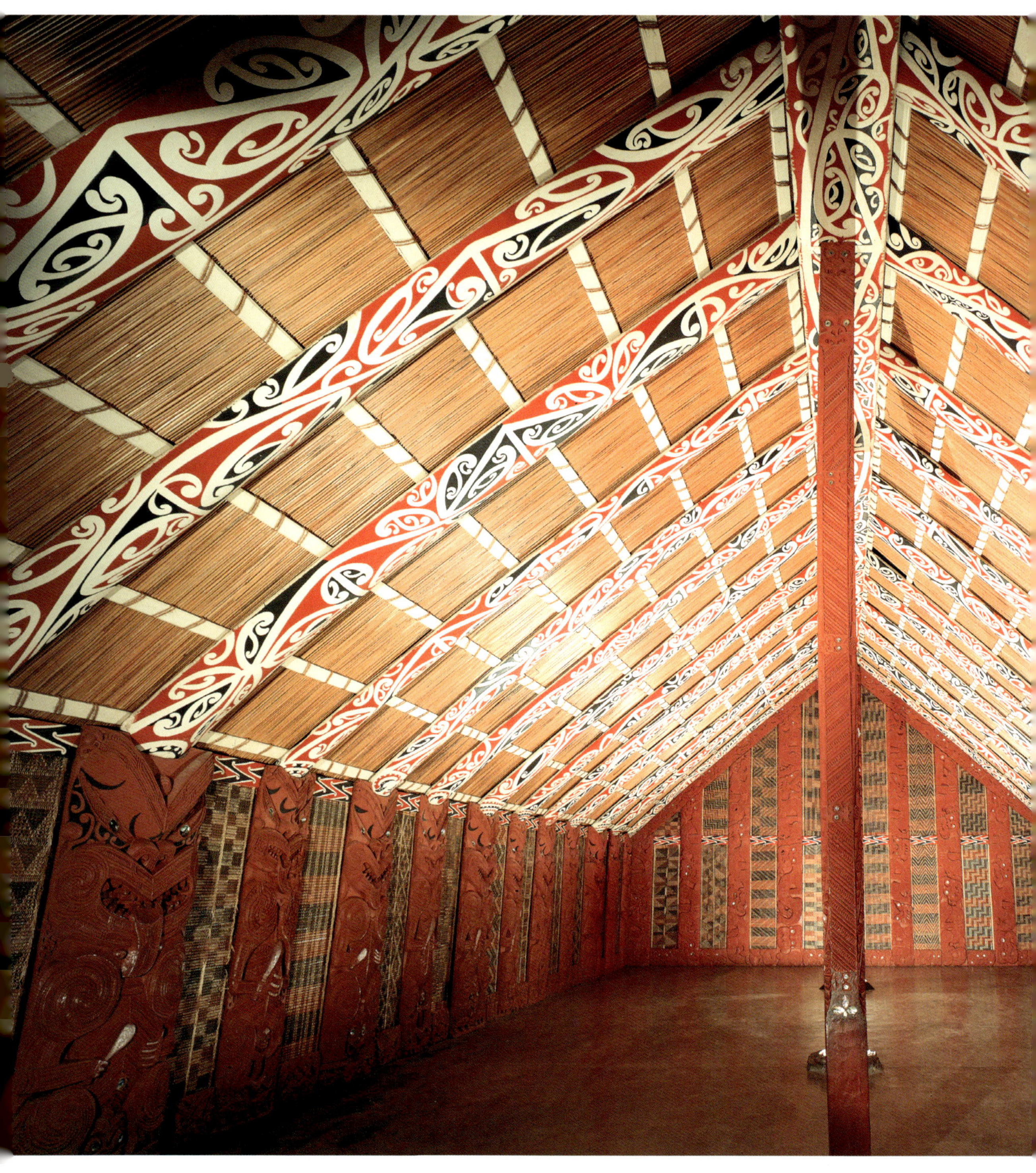

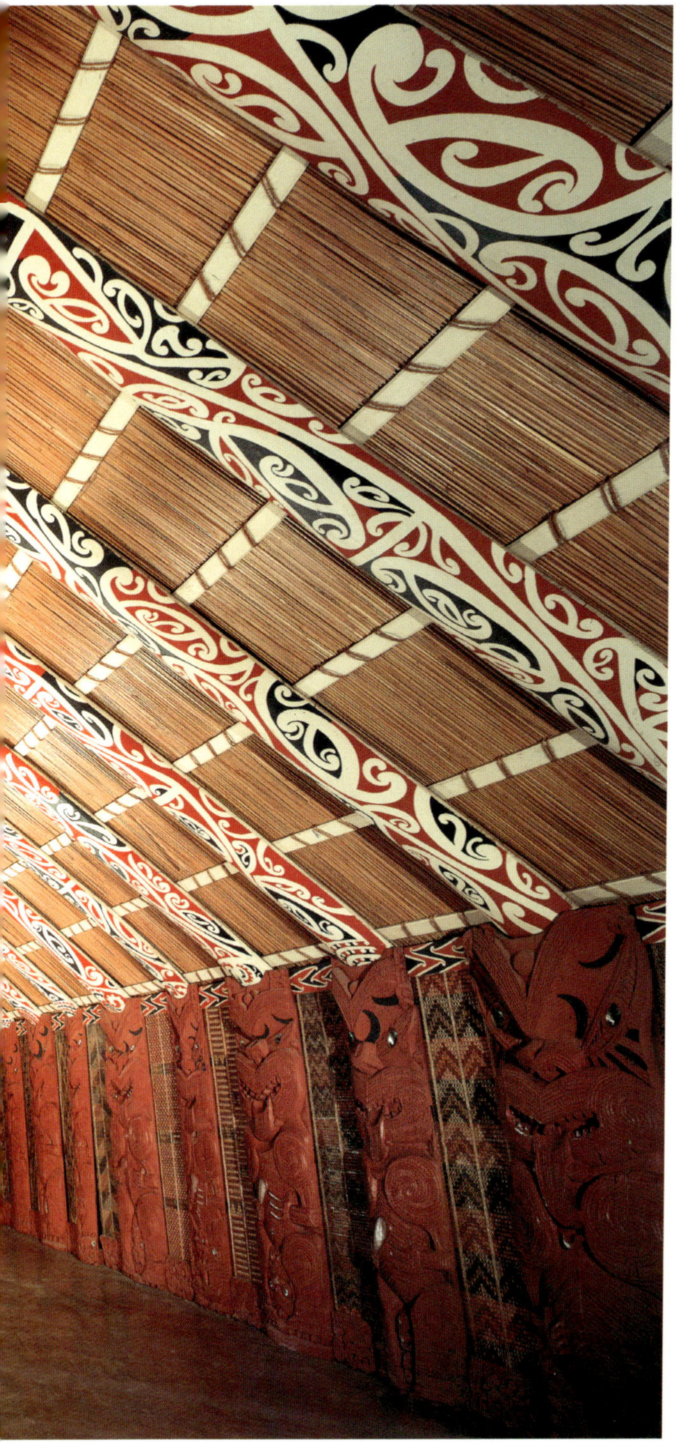

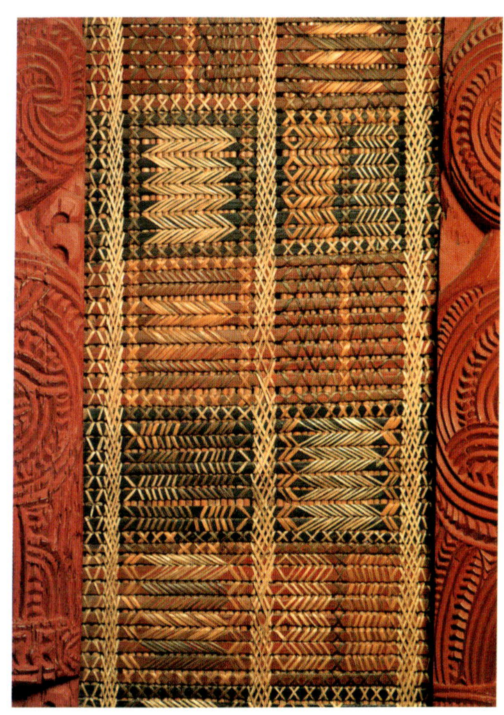

2A & 2B. tukutuku (lattice wall panel) from
Hotunui meeting house & interior of Hotunui
meeting house
built at Parawai in 1878 by Ngati Awa craftspeople,
under the leadership of Wepiha Apanui
Auckland Museum Tamaki Paenga Hira AM 49394
presented to the museum in 1929

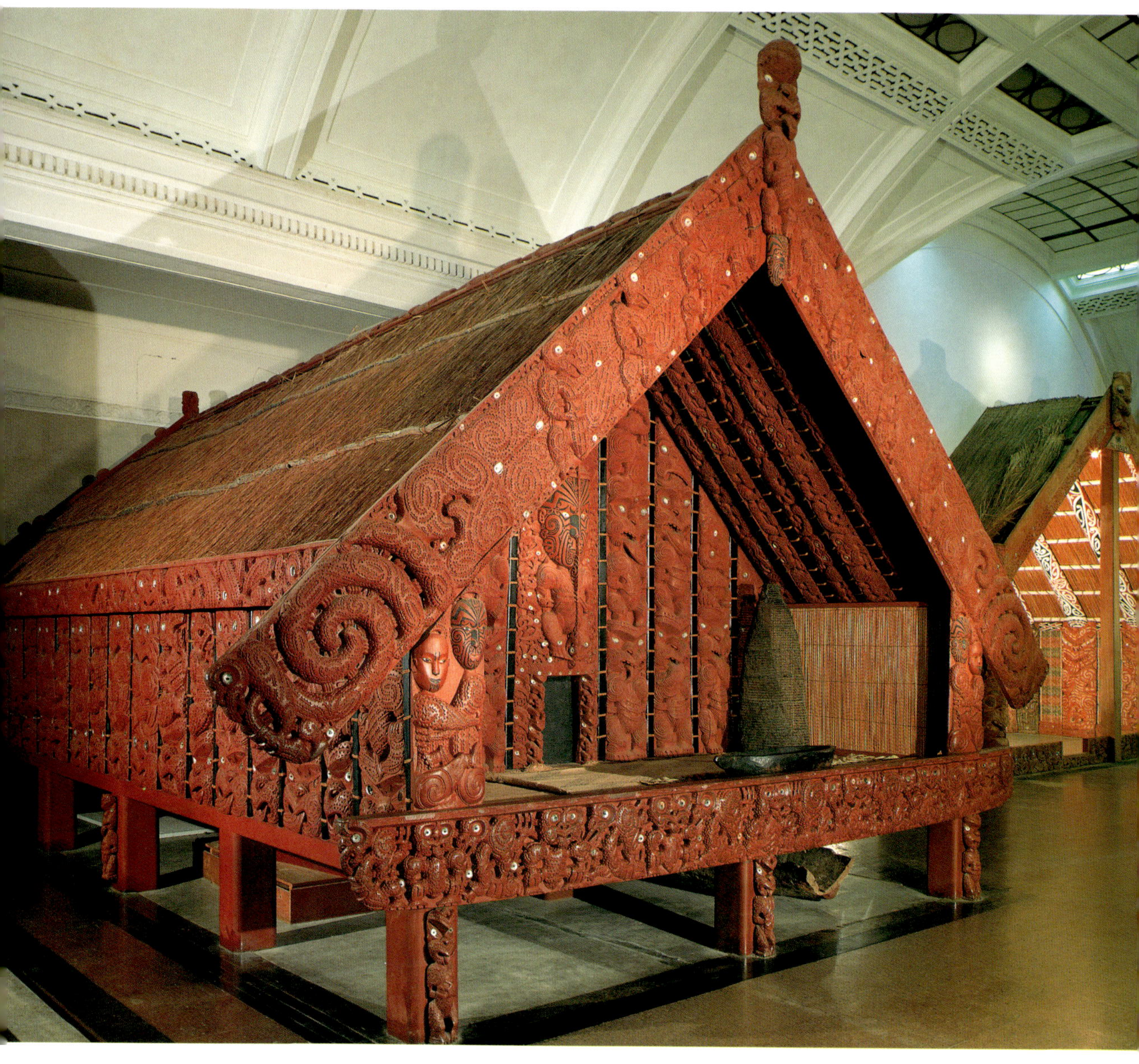

2C & 2D. Te Puawai-o-Te Arawa pataka (storehouse)
10.5 m (l) x 6.00 m (w)
wood, shell
built at Maketu in the early 1870s
Auckland Museum Tamaki Paenga Hira AM 151
purchased from the Ngati Pikiao rangatira (tribal chief) Te Pohika Taranui in 1894

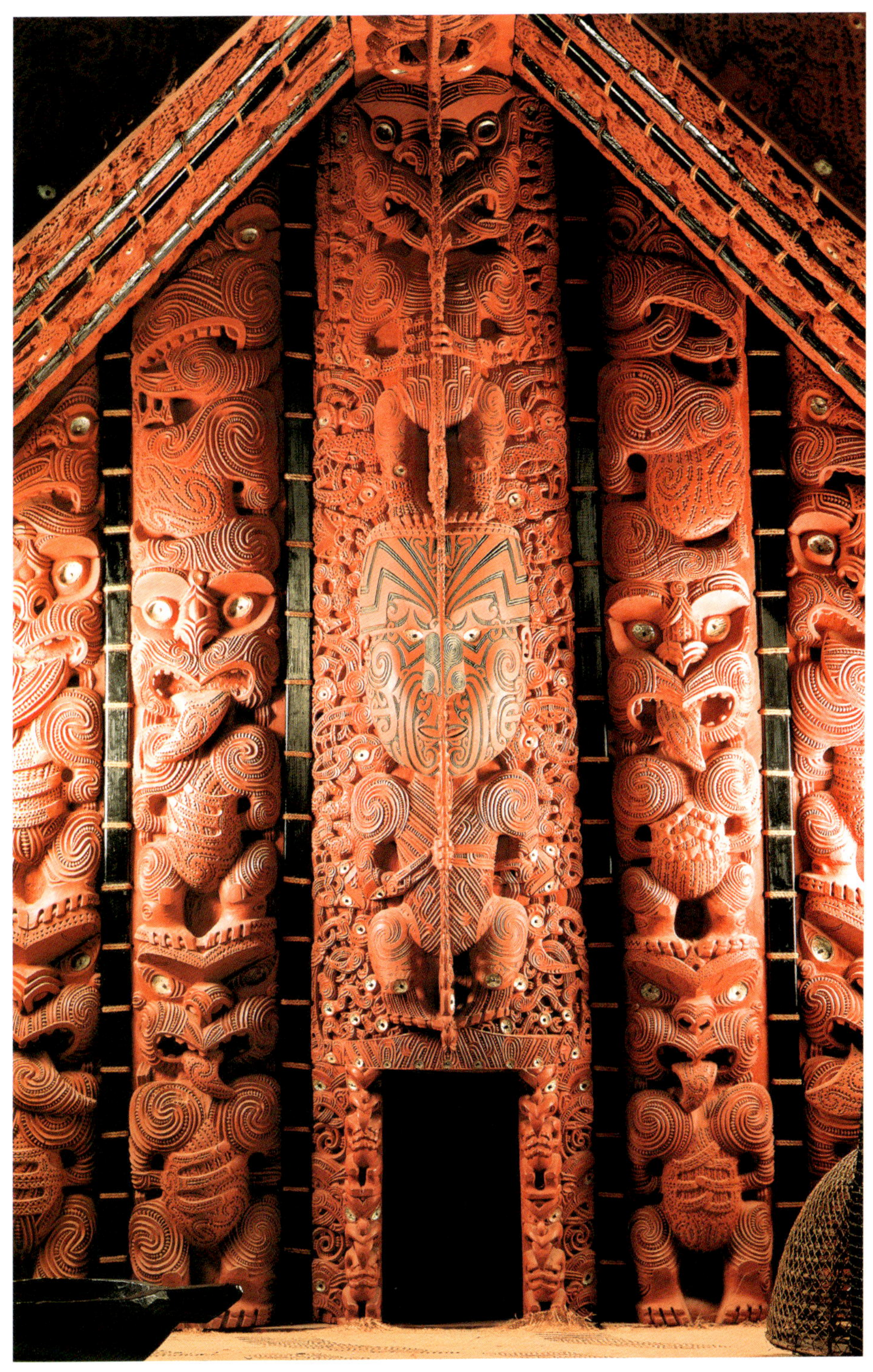

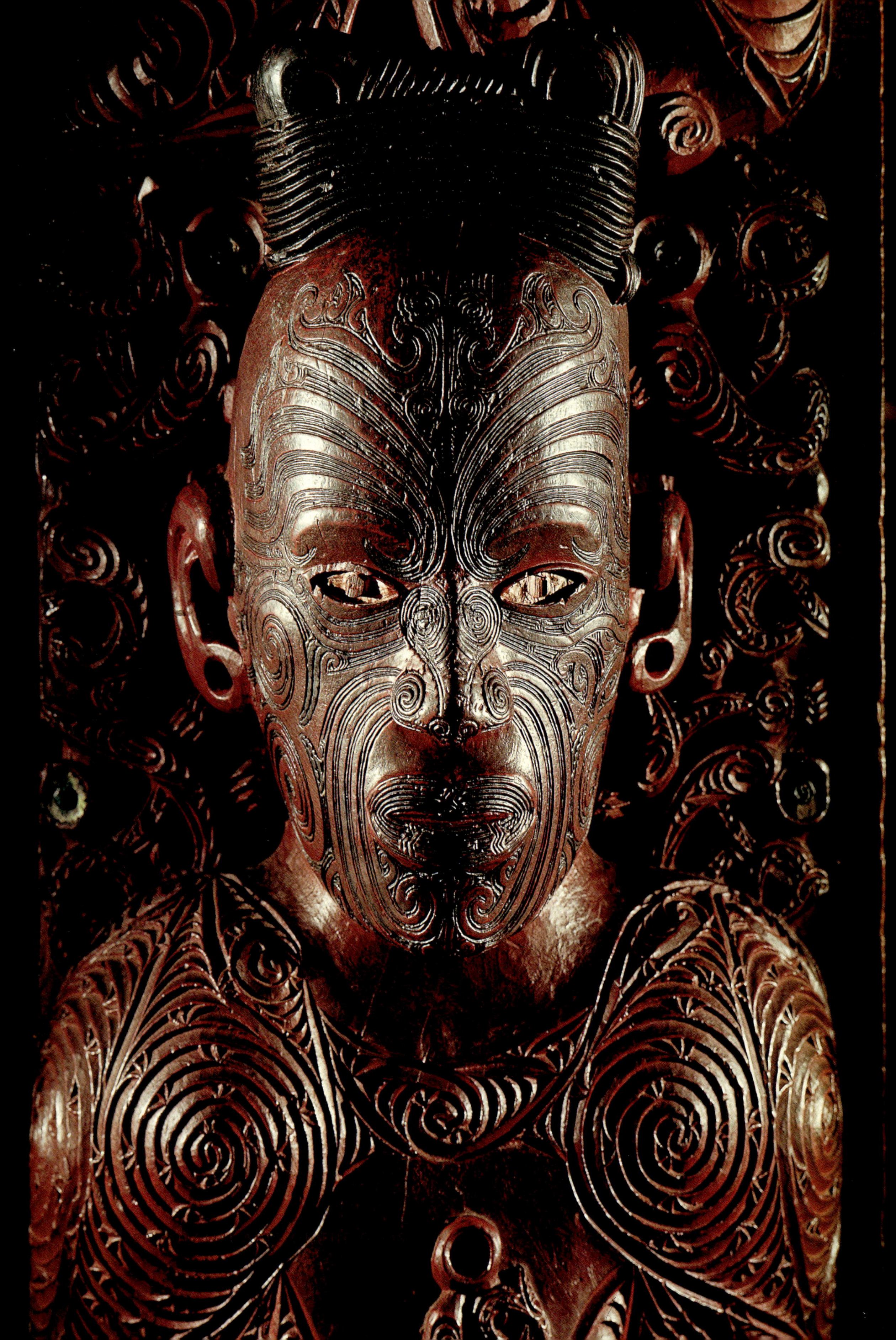

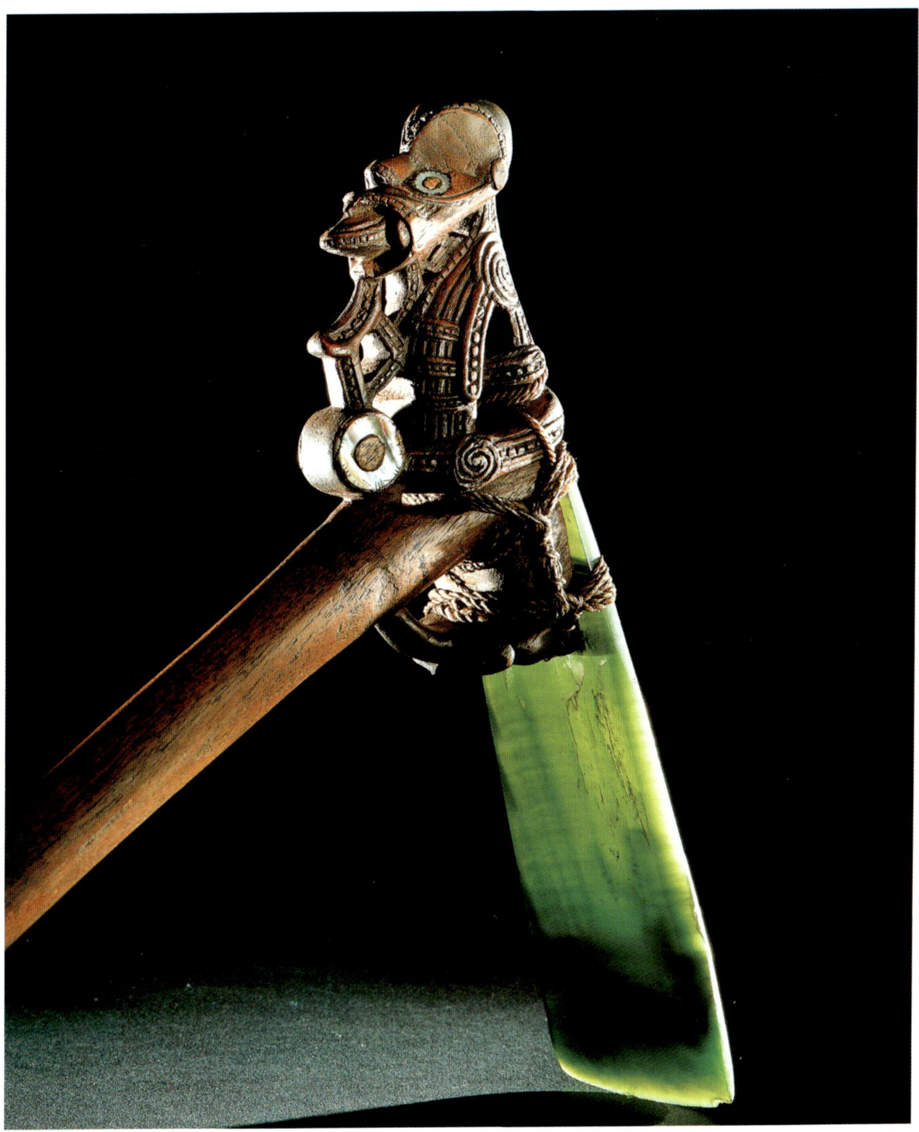

‹ 2E. poupou (wall post)
from Te Hau-ki-Turanga meeting house
1.08 m
wood
built at Turanga in the early 1840s
by Raharuhi Rukupo
Museum of New Zealand Te Papa Tongarewa

⌃ 2F. toki poutangata
(ceremonial adze)
440 mm
wood, pounamu (greenstone,
New Zealand jade), flax
Otago Museum D 51.509

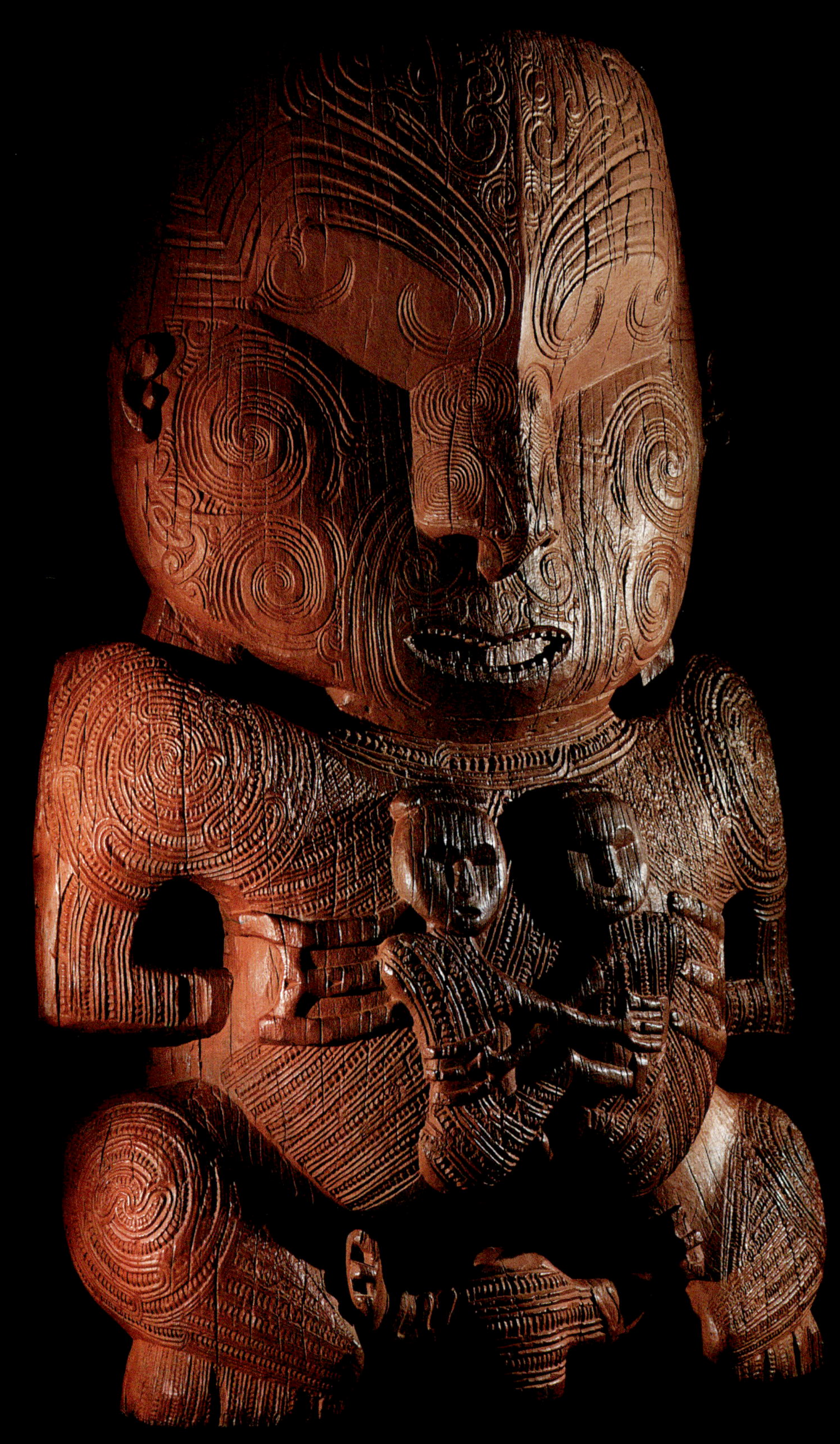

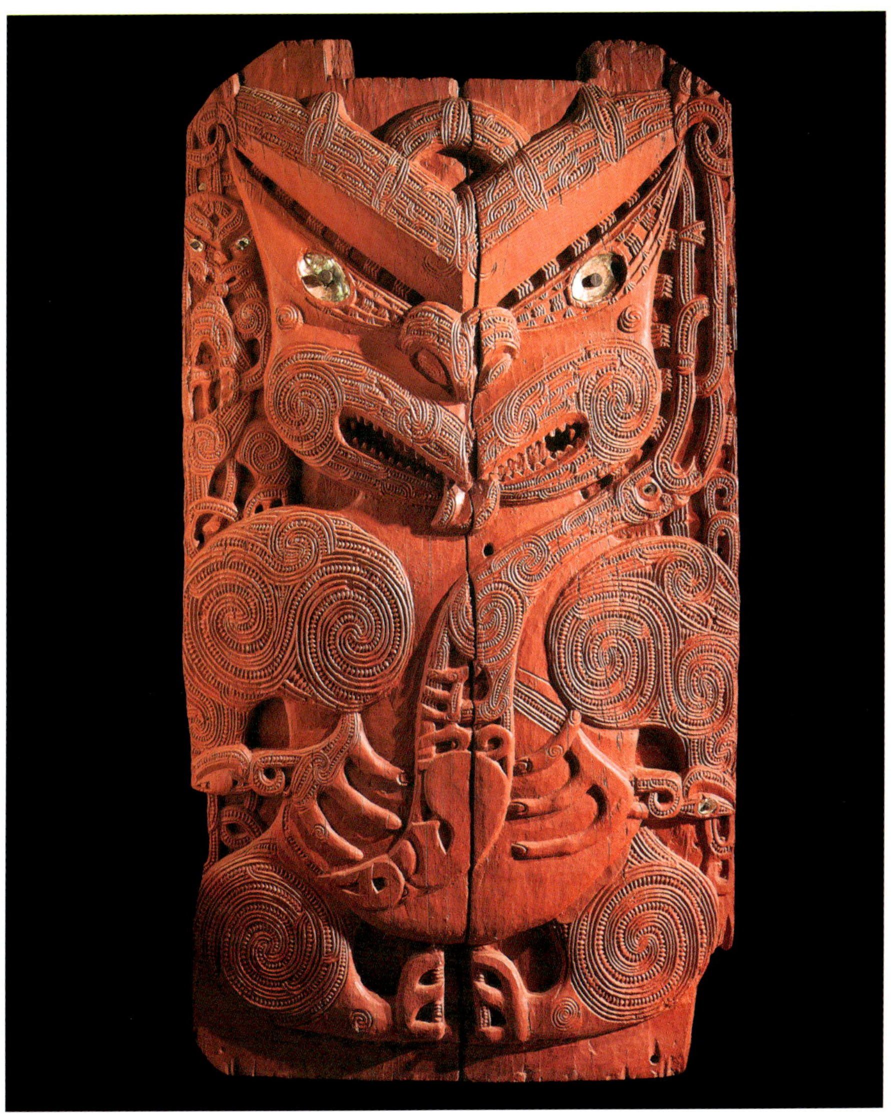

‹ 2G. 'Pukaki' kuwaha (gateway)
1.96 m
totara wood
carved c. 1836 by Taupua Te Whanoa of the
Ngati Whakaue tribe for Pukeroa pa, in Rotorua
Rotorua District Council
formerly Auckland Museum Tamaki Paenga Hira
presented by Ngati Whakaue in 1877

^ 2H. poupou (wall post)
1.46 m
Lake Taupo
wood
Auckland Museum Tamaki Paenga
Hira AM 4719

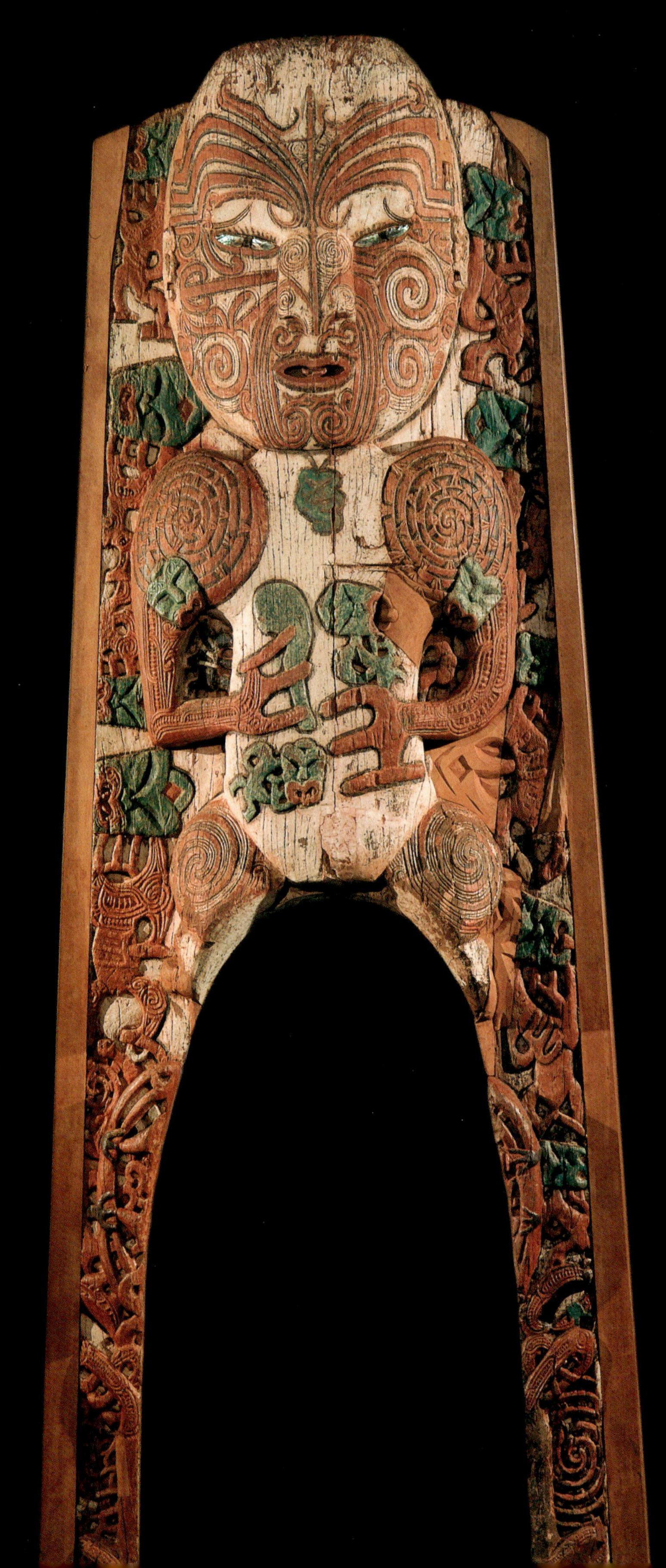

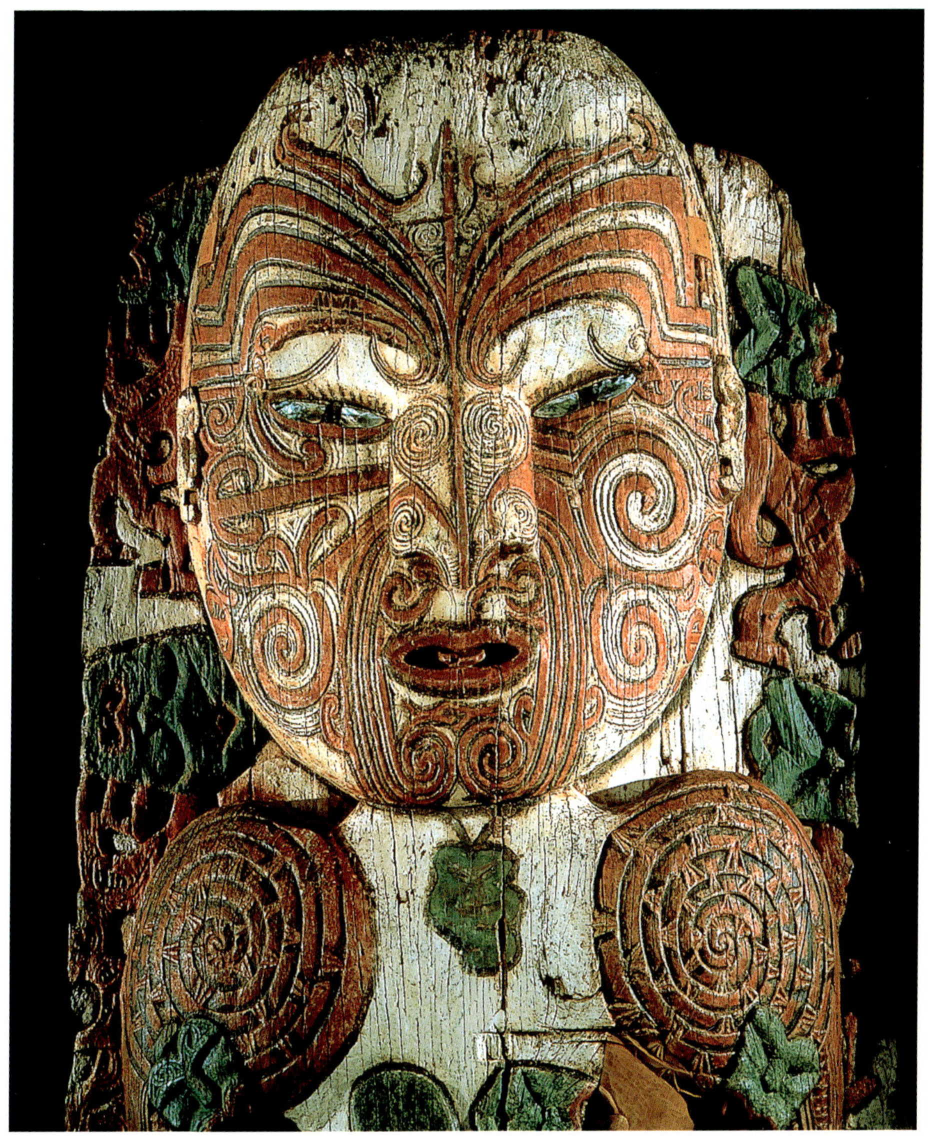

21. 'Tiki' kuwaha (gateway)

3.80 m

wood

carved in the early nineteenth century by Te Umanui

of the Ngati Whakaue tribe for Muruika pa, in Rotorua

Auckland Museum Tamaki Paenga Hira AM 160

presented by the New Zealand government

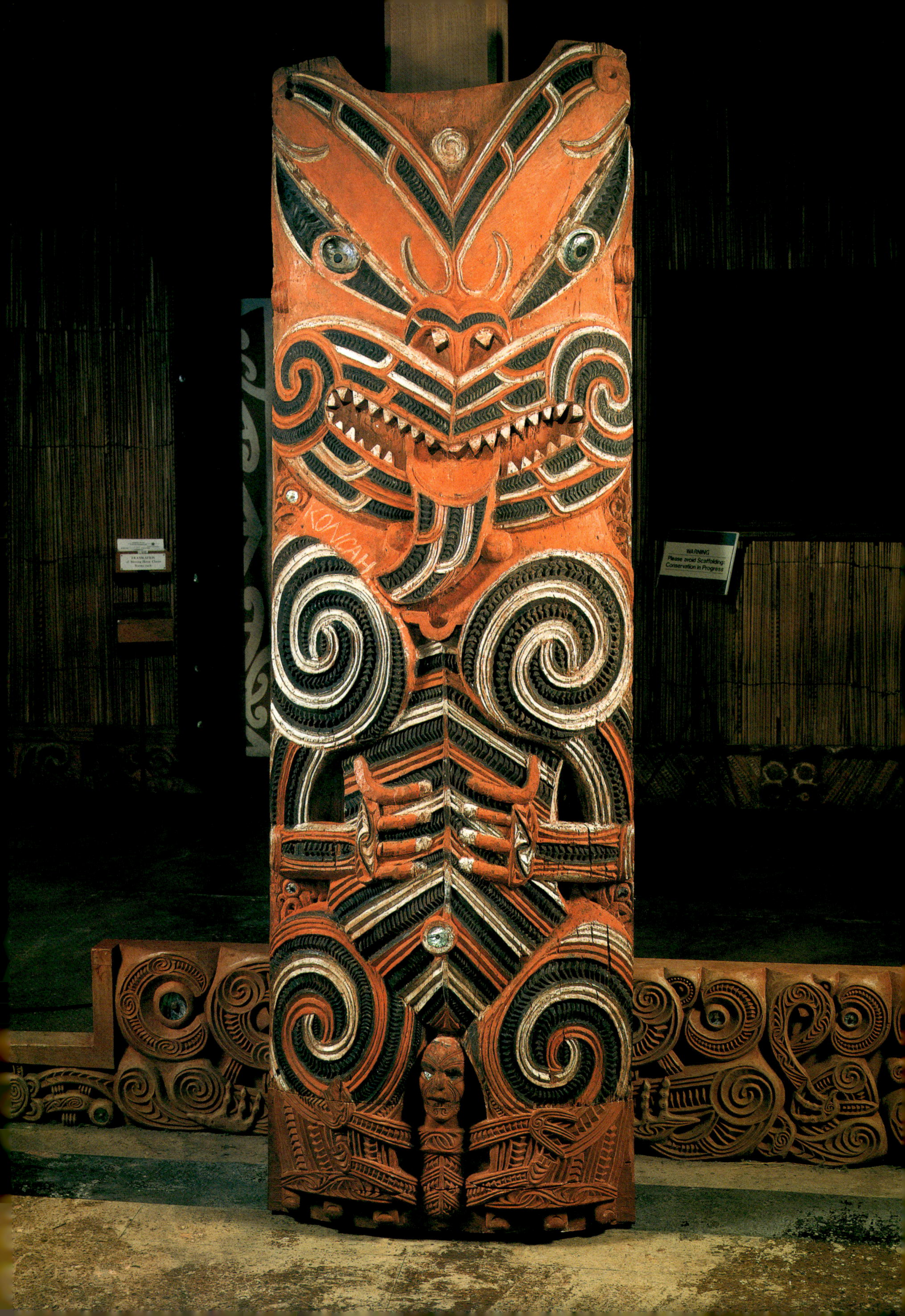

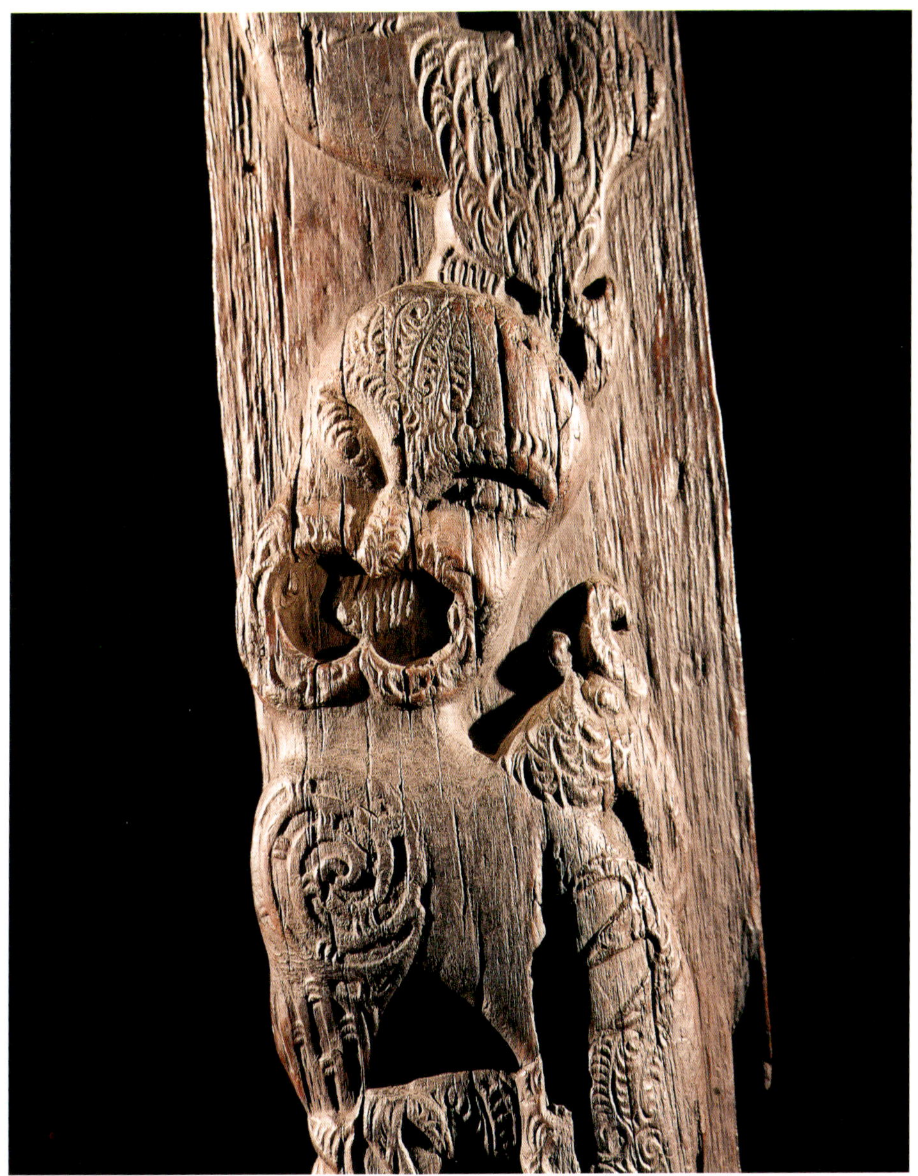

‹ 2J. poupou (ancestral wall post figure) from the
Hotunui meeting house
built at Parawai in 1878 by Ngati Awa craftspeople,
under the leadership of Wepiha Apanui
Auckland Museum Tamaki Paenga Hira
AM 49394
presented to the museum in 1929

⌃ 2K. central detail of a whakawae
(door jamb) of a storehouse
1080 mm x 230 mm
wood
attributed to the Awanui area
Far North Regional Museum 819

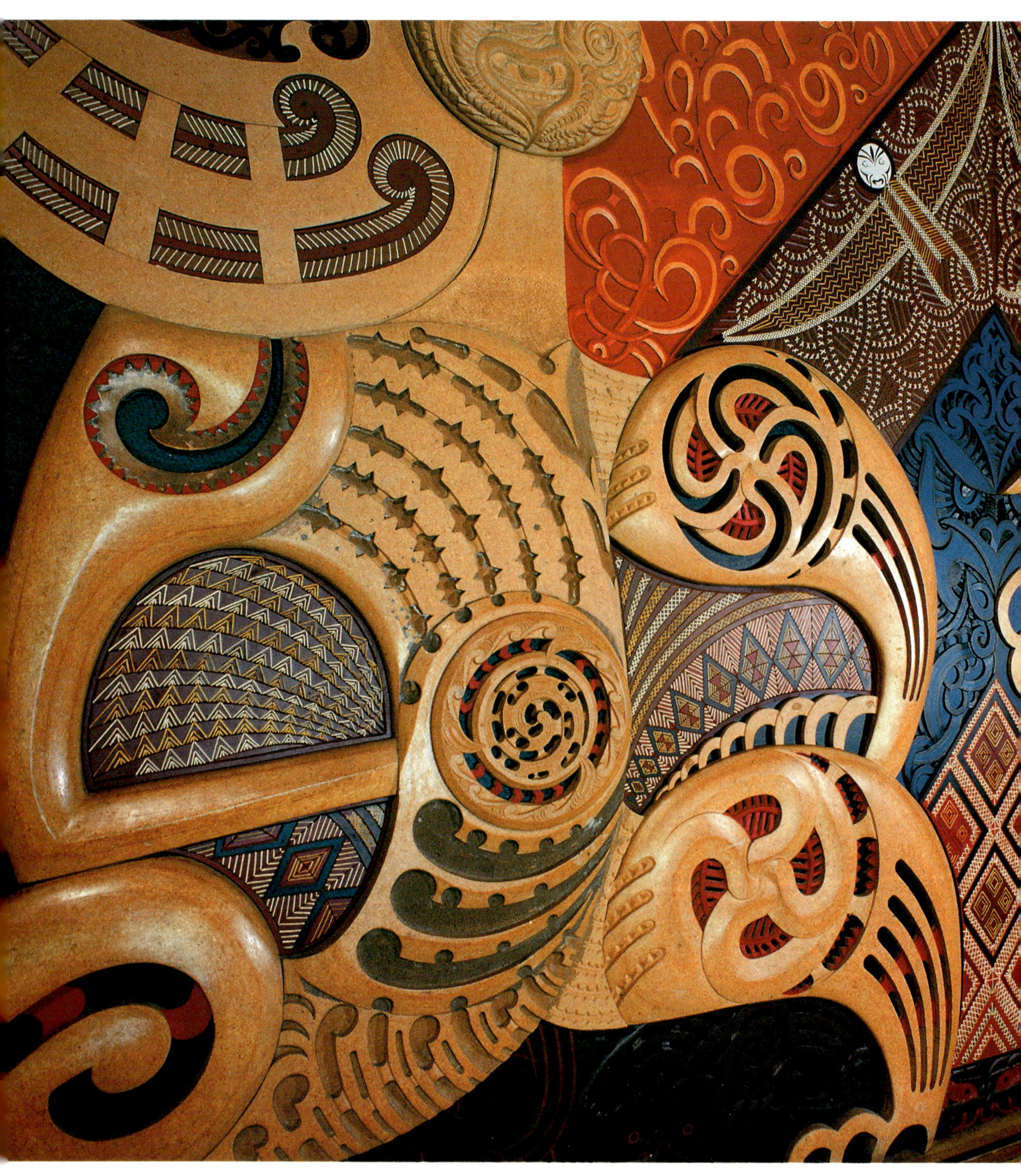

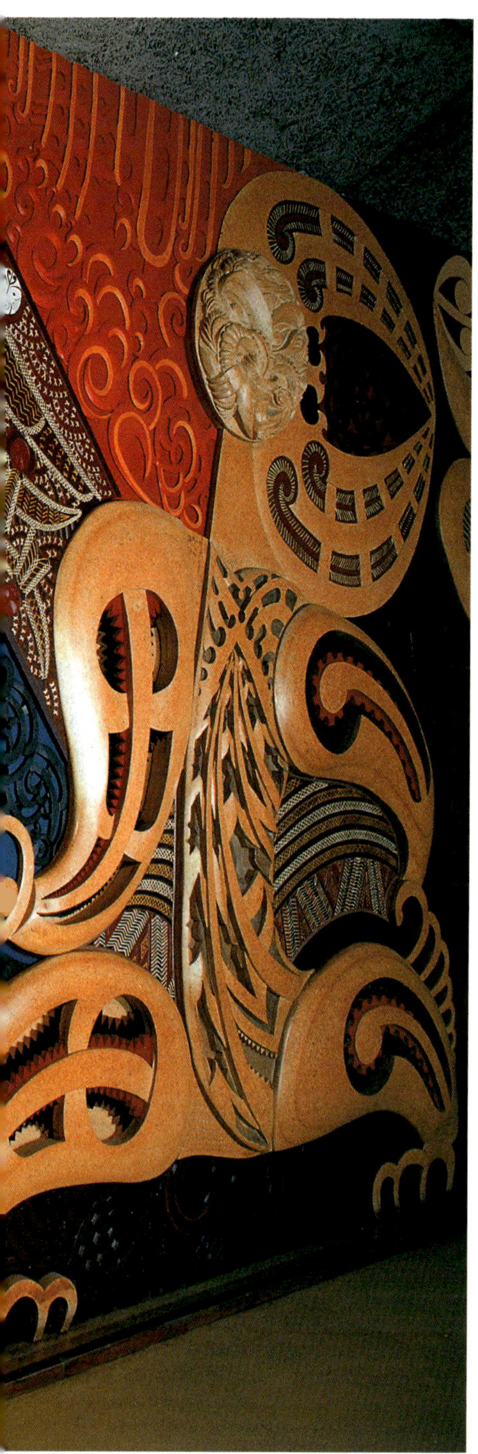

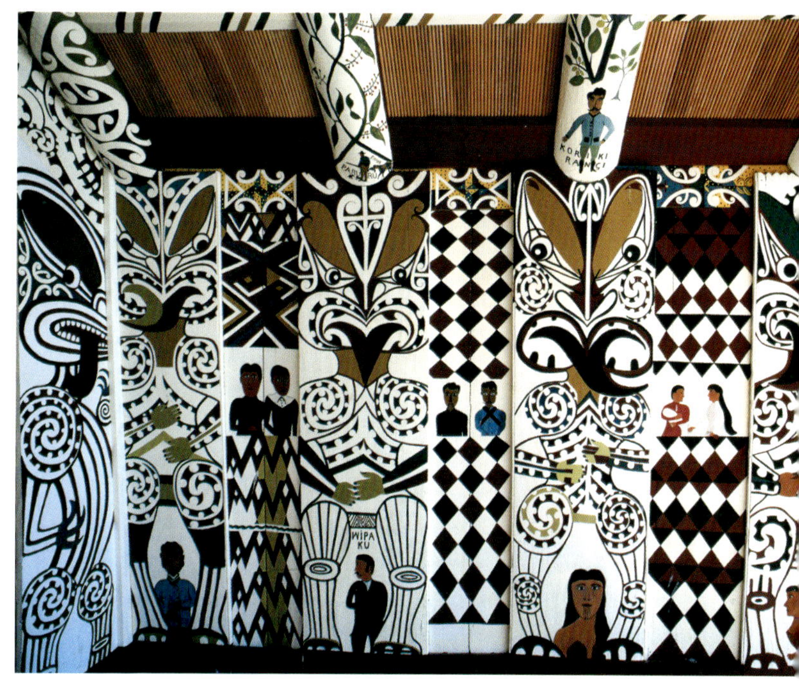

▲2L. porch wall of Rongopai meeting house
built at Waituhi in 1887 by Ringatu adherents

◄2M. 'Te Whanaketanga o nga iwi o Tainui'
mural
created for the Kimiora Centre, Turangawaewae
marae, in 1976, under the leadership of
Paratene Matchitt

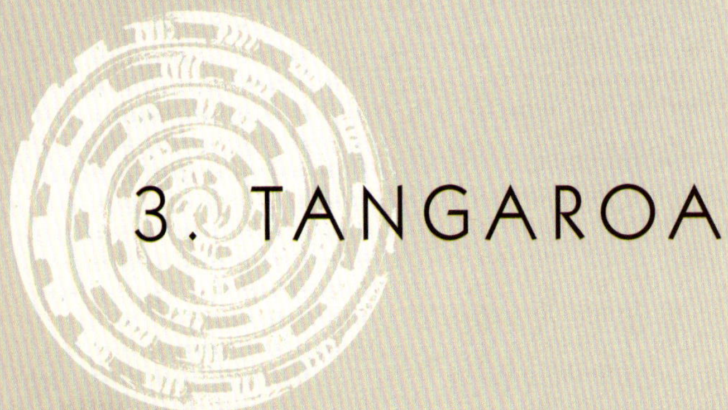

3. TANGAROA

Many narratives identify Tangaroa as the son of Papatuanuku (although in others he is her first husband) and they generally describe him as the god of the sea and its tides; father to fish, taniwha (water spirits), marine mammals, seabirds, pounamu (greenstone, New Zealand jade) and reptiles; and patron of fishers.

Tangaroa's taniwha children include whales, sharks, eels and supernatural serpents that live in the ocean, rivers and lakes and sometimes in the land and air. They can be benevolent, and act as guardians and protectors, but are also associated with evil and danger. In some narratives they are Tane's descendants, not Tangaroa's. One type of taniwha can swallow men and boats through a long tubular tongue, and is represented in central and eastern North Island wood carving as the character known as 'marakihau', a humanoid figure from the waist-up with a fish tail. Paneiraira, a taniwha associated with the Tainui vessel's migratory journey from Hawaiki, has been depicted as a marakihau (pl. 3A) even though he is remembered as a guardian in Tainui ancestral narratives. With the arrival of Pakeha (Europeans) the image of marakihau was influenced by stories of mermaids, as can be seen in the marakihau's illustration as a woman in late nineteenth and early twentieth century naturalistic wood carvings (pl. 3B).

Tangaroa and Tane became enemies after the separation of their parents and their animosity is reinforced by natural disasters involving land and water, and also human consumption of sea creatures. As children of Tane, fishers crafted intricate lures, hooks and floats (pls

3C & 3D), from wood, bone, shell and stone — sometimes decorated with the faces and figures of ancestors — to catch Tangaroa's children. It is thought that the practice of wearing these utilitarian objects as pendants, to keep them safe and at hand, eventually led to the development of hei matau (pl. 3E), or stylised fishhook necklaces. The ivory of sea creatures is also used to make jewellery, such as the rei niho (pl. 3F), featuring a multitude of bodies, and the eel-eyed rei puta (pl. 3G), both pendants customarily fashioned from whale tooth.

Human intervention into Tangaroa's domain is by way of waka (canoes), which have varied in form from simple small unadorned dug-outs, to reed craft, to wider-hulled waka taua (war canoes; pl. 3H) adorned with tauihu (pl. 3I & 3J), haumi (bow cover; pl. 3K), rauawa (gunnels), taurapa (pls 3L & 3M), and tiheru (bailer; pl. 3N) wood carvings. The legendary ancestor Rata made the first waka, and stories of its manufacture reinforce the significance of Tane as progenitor of timber (see p. 14). A waka cutting a path through the water is, therefore, replaying a conflict that has its roots in the Creation story and the animosity between Tangaroa and Tane. Indeed, the god of war, Tumatauenga, is often carved onto the front of tauihu as a reminder of this and other disputes (pl. 3I).

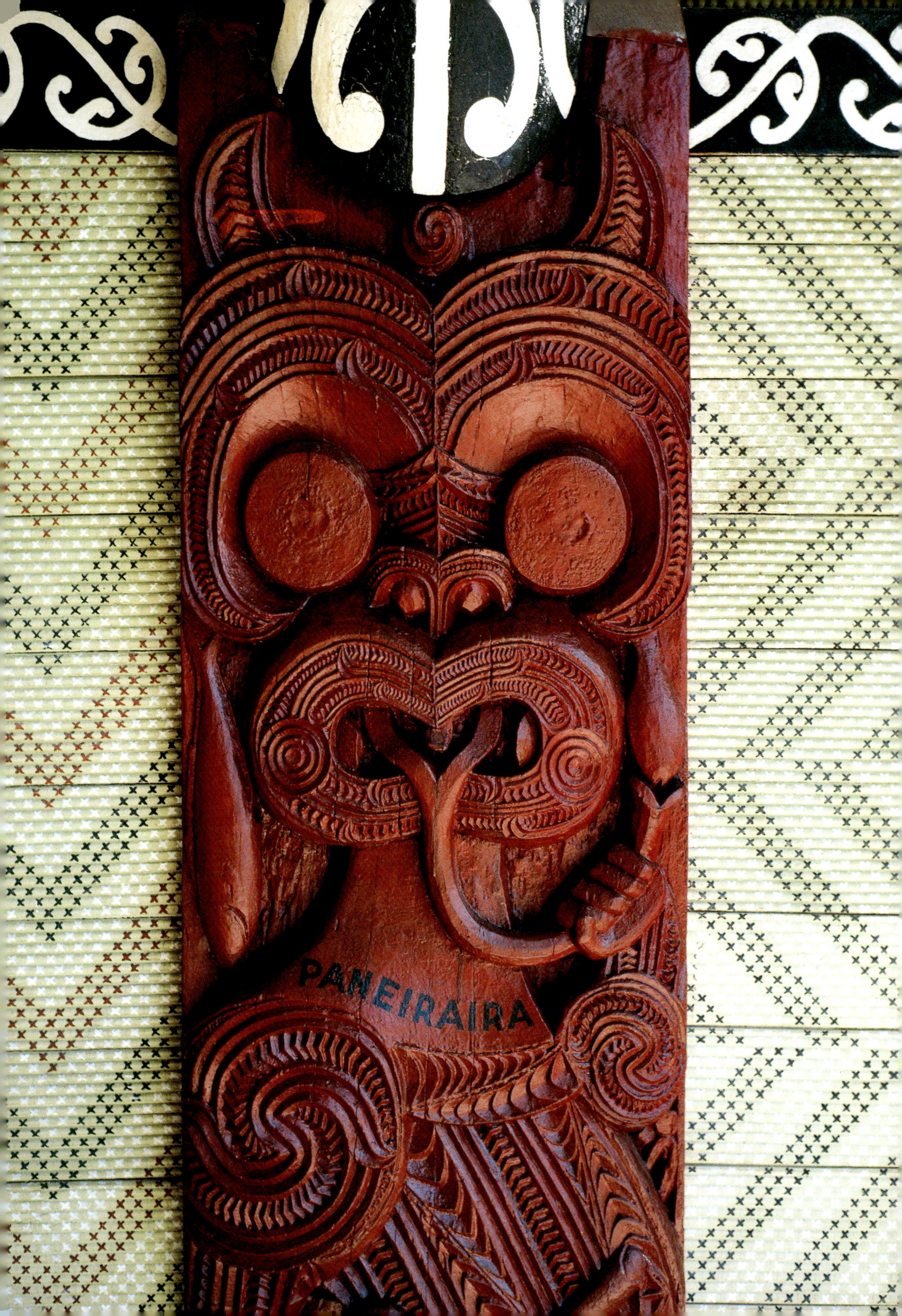
PANEIRAIRA

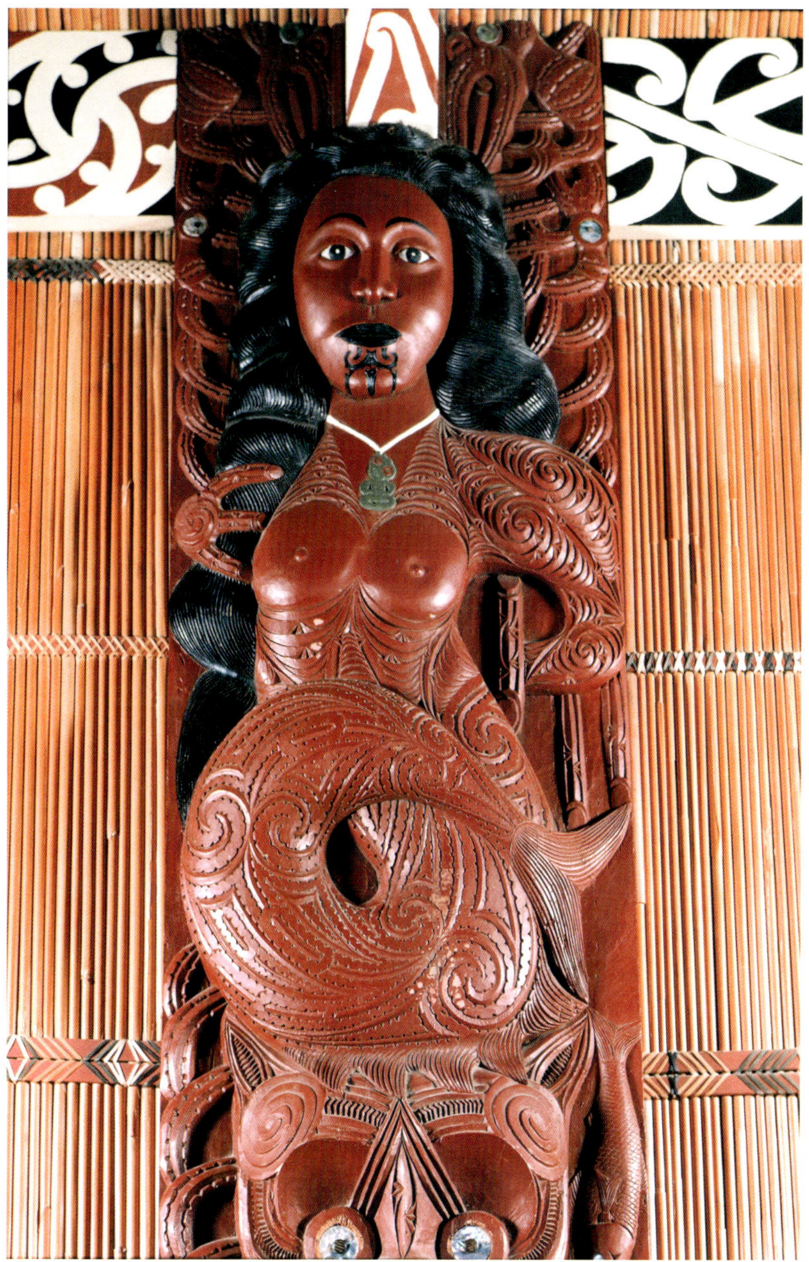

<3A. 'Paneiraira', poupou (wall panel)

wood

probably from the porch of the

Te Tokanganui-a-Noho meeting house, Te Kuiti

^ 3B. poupou (wall panel)

wood

Rautahi marae, Kawerau

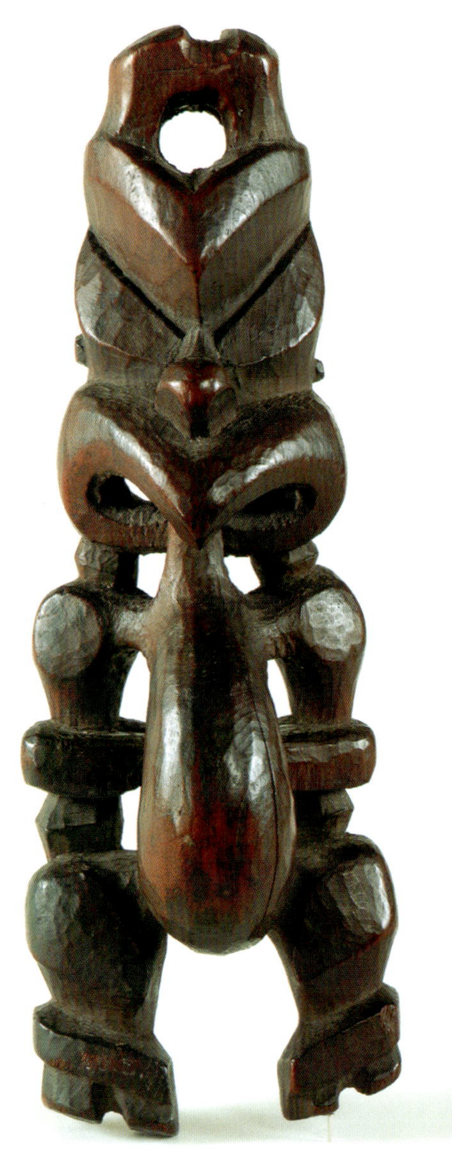

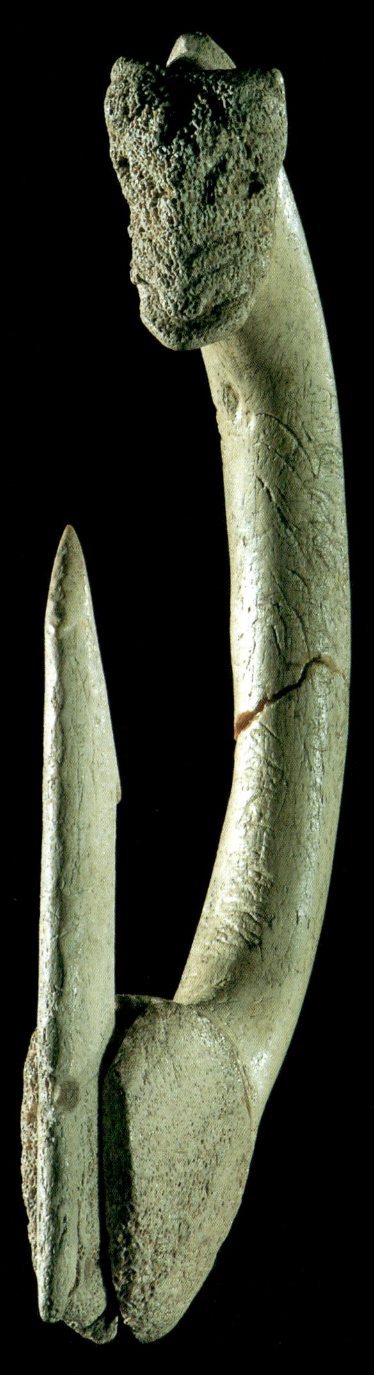

^ 3C. matau (fishhook)
155 mm
bone
Southland Museum and Art
Gallery B 64.153

‹ 3D. poito (fishing float)
250 mm (h) x 90 mm (w)
wood
from the Lake Rotoiti district
Auckland Museum Tamaki
Paenga Hira AM 40
purchased from the
Gilbert Mair collection

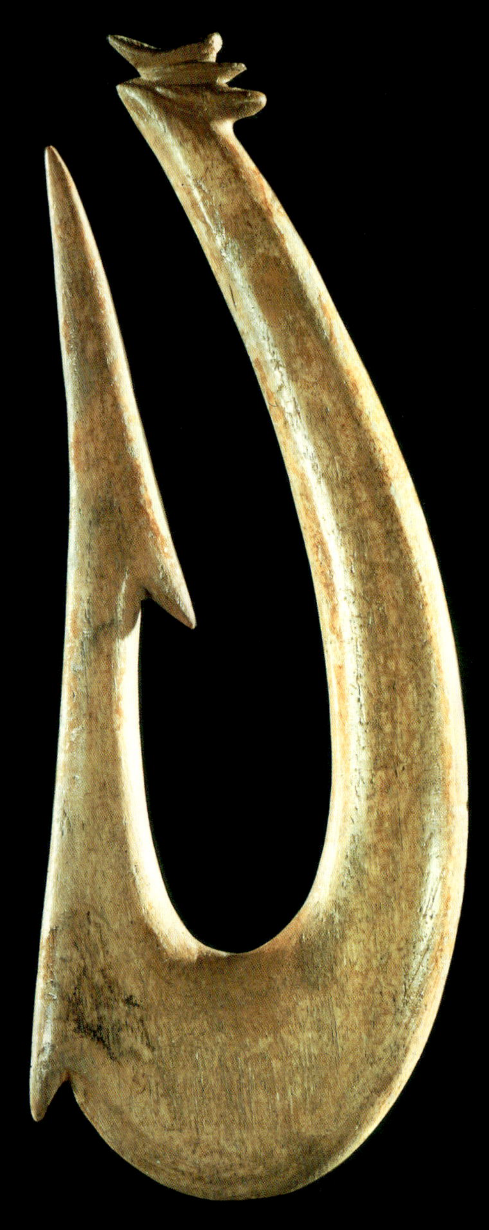

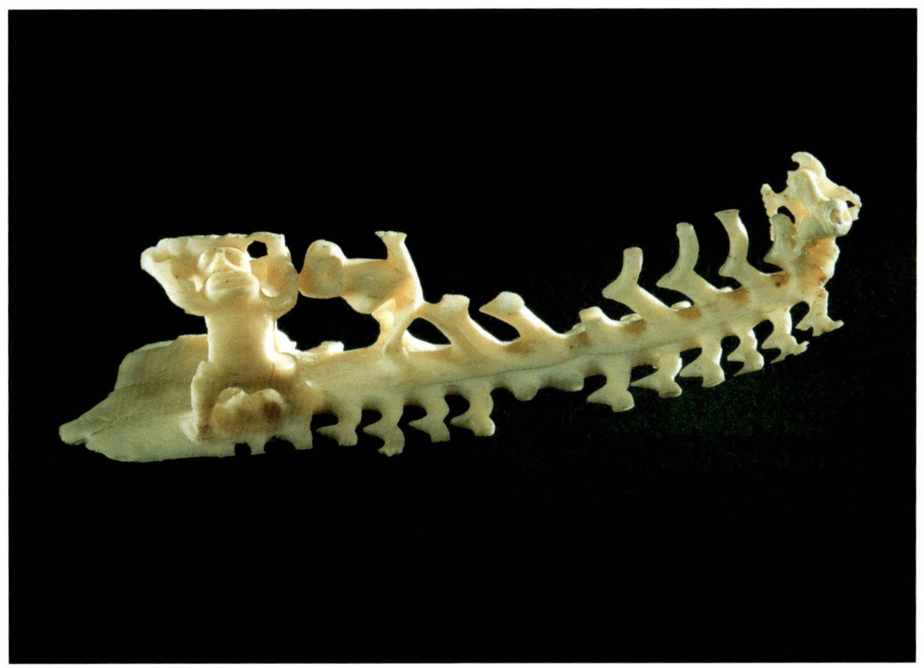

‹ 3E. hei matau (fishhook necklace)

160 mm

bone

from the Papanui Inlet

Otago Museum D 27.257

formerly John White collection

⌃ 3F. rei niho (whale tooth pendant)

126 mm (l) x 36 mm (w)

whaletooth

found in sand dunes at the Whangamumu

Harbour in 1895

Auckland Museum Tamaki Paenga Hira

AM 21859

formerly Lushington collection

› 3G. rei puta (pendant)

162 mm

whaletooth, flax fibre

Hancock Museum, Newcastle-on-Tyne C675

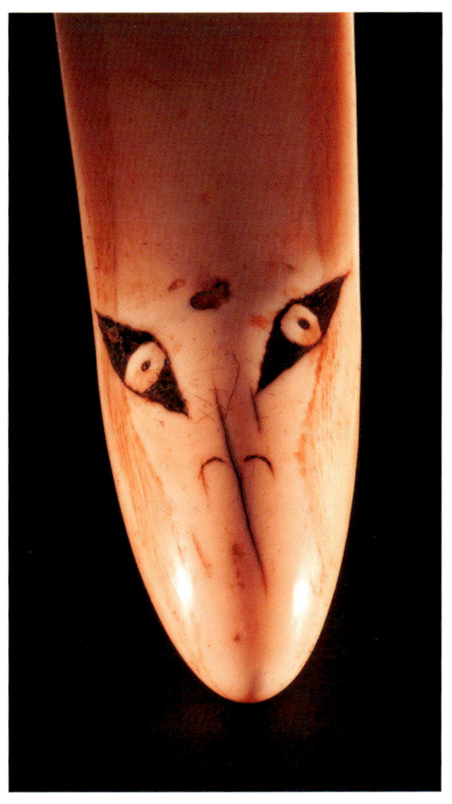

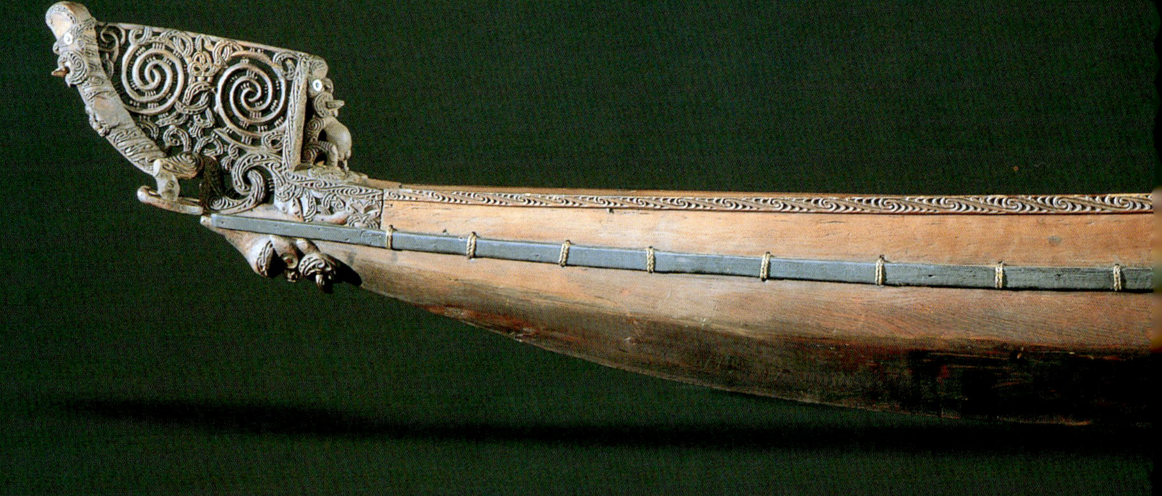

3H. model waka taua (war canoe)
2.450 m (l) x 311 mm (w)
wood
Auckland Museum Tamaki Paenga Hira AM 44117

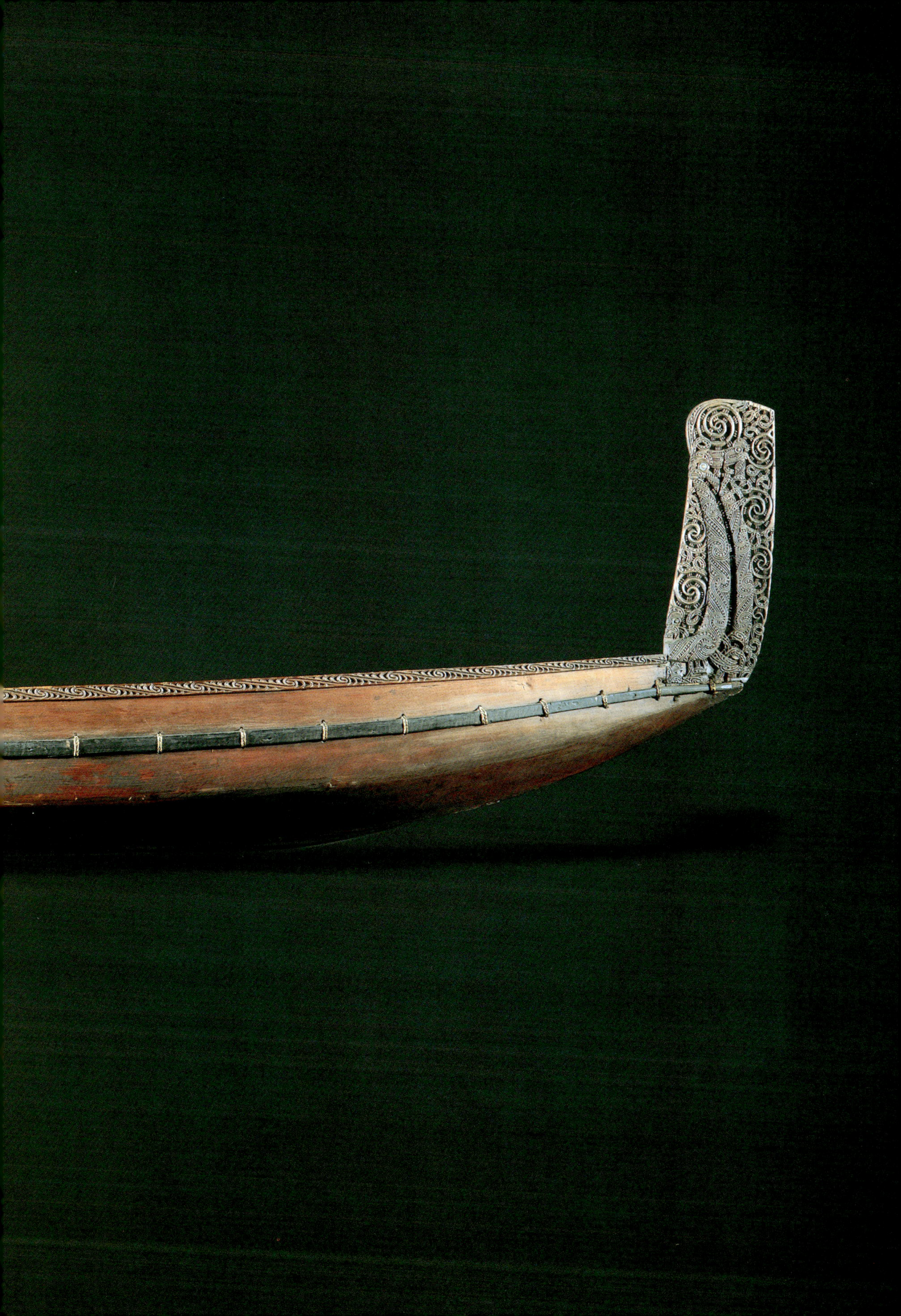

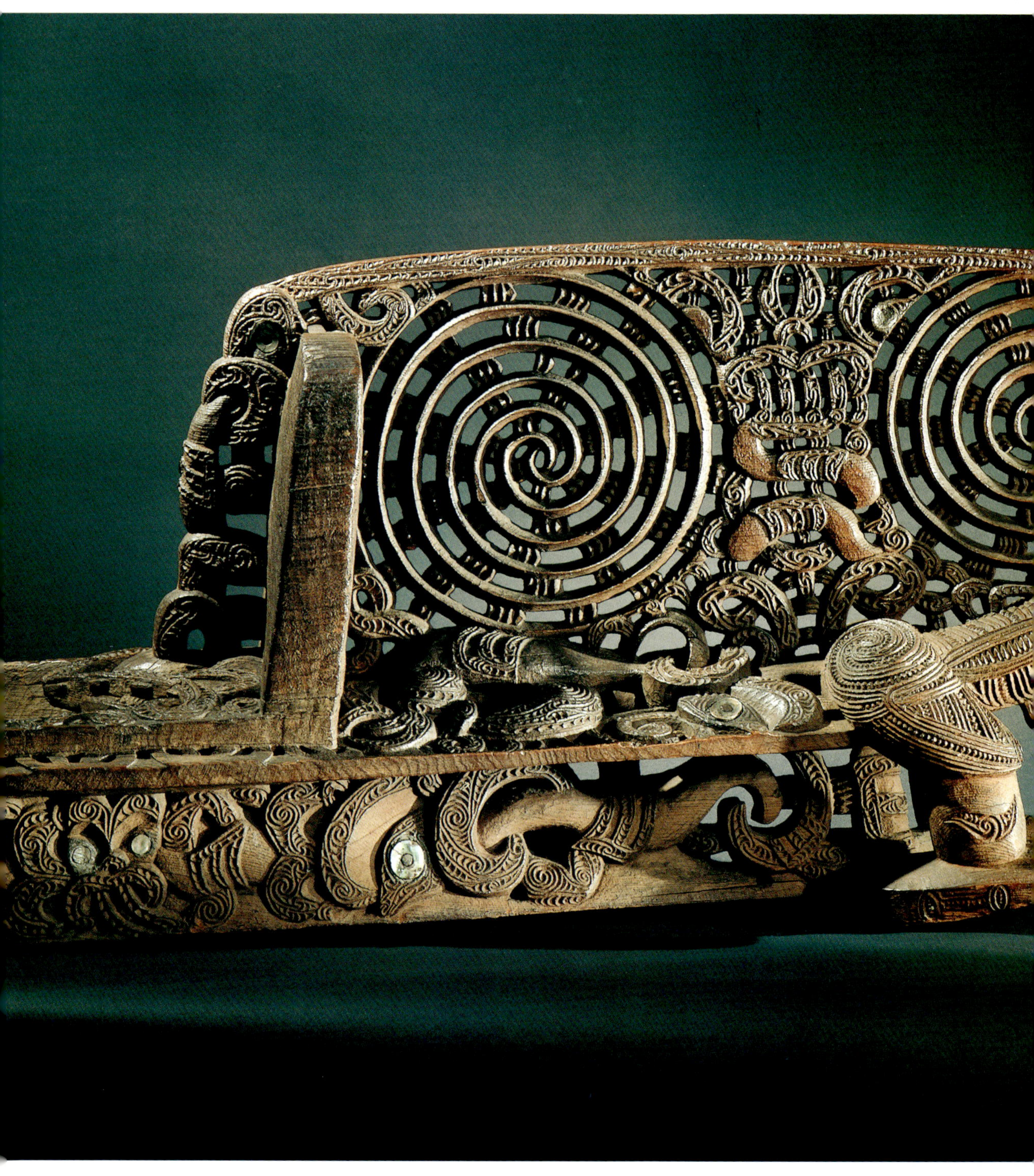

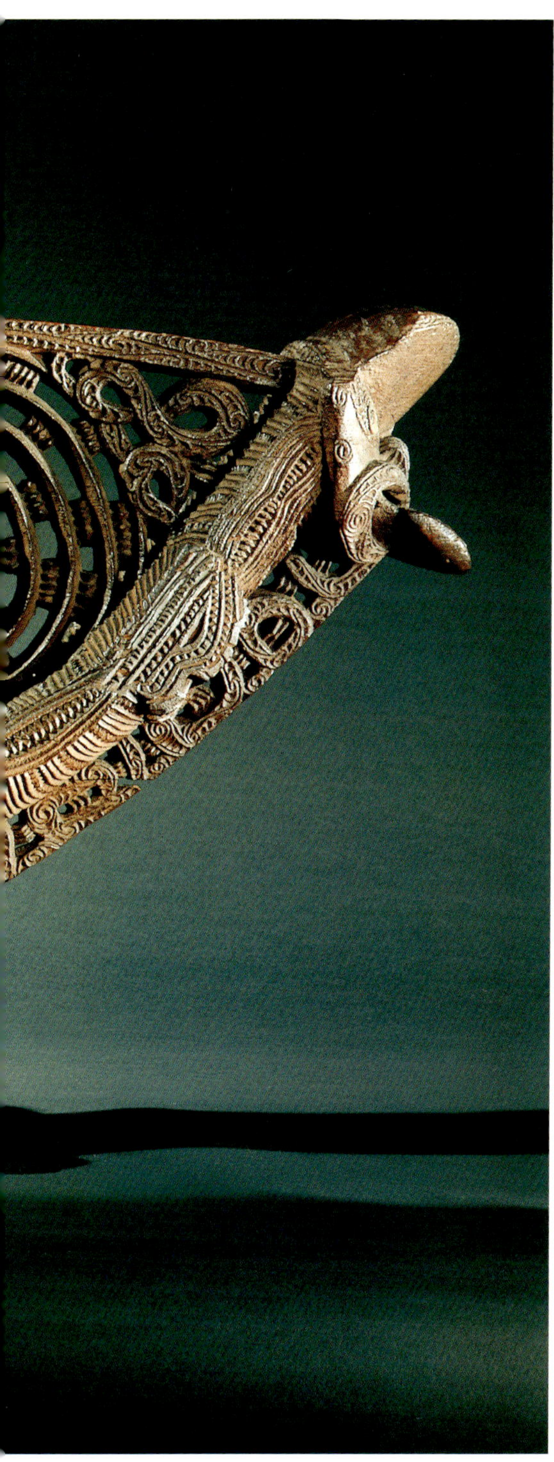

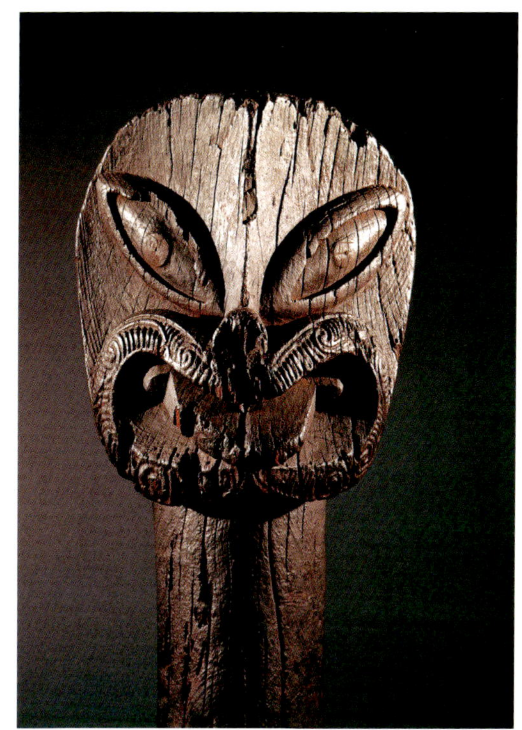

‹ 3I. tauihu (canoe prow)
500 mm (h) x 1185 mm (w) x 410 mm (d)
wood, paua shell
Museum of New Zealand Te Papa
Tongarewa WE 1202
formerly K. A. Webster collection,
formerly Enys collection

^ 3J. tauihu (canoe figurehead)
540 mm
wood
Otago Museum L71.68
on loan from Auckland Museum Tamaki
Paenga Hira AM 6156

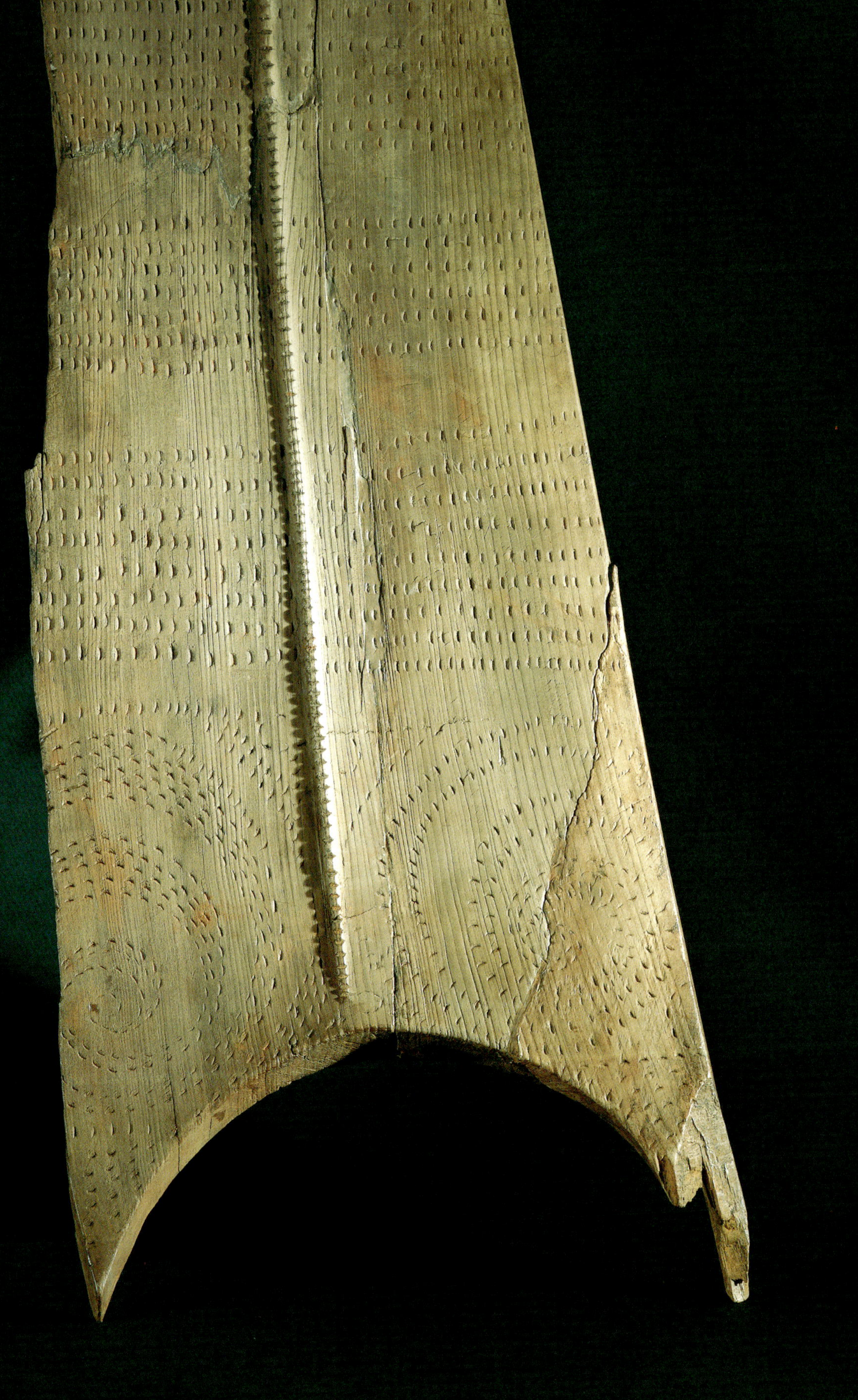

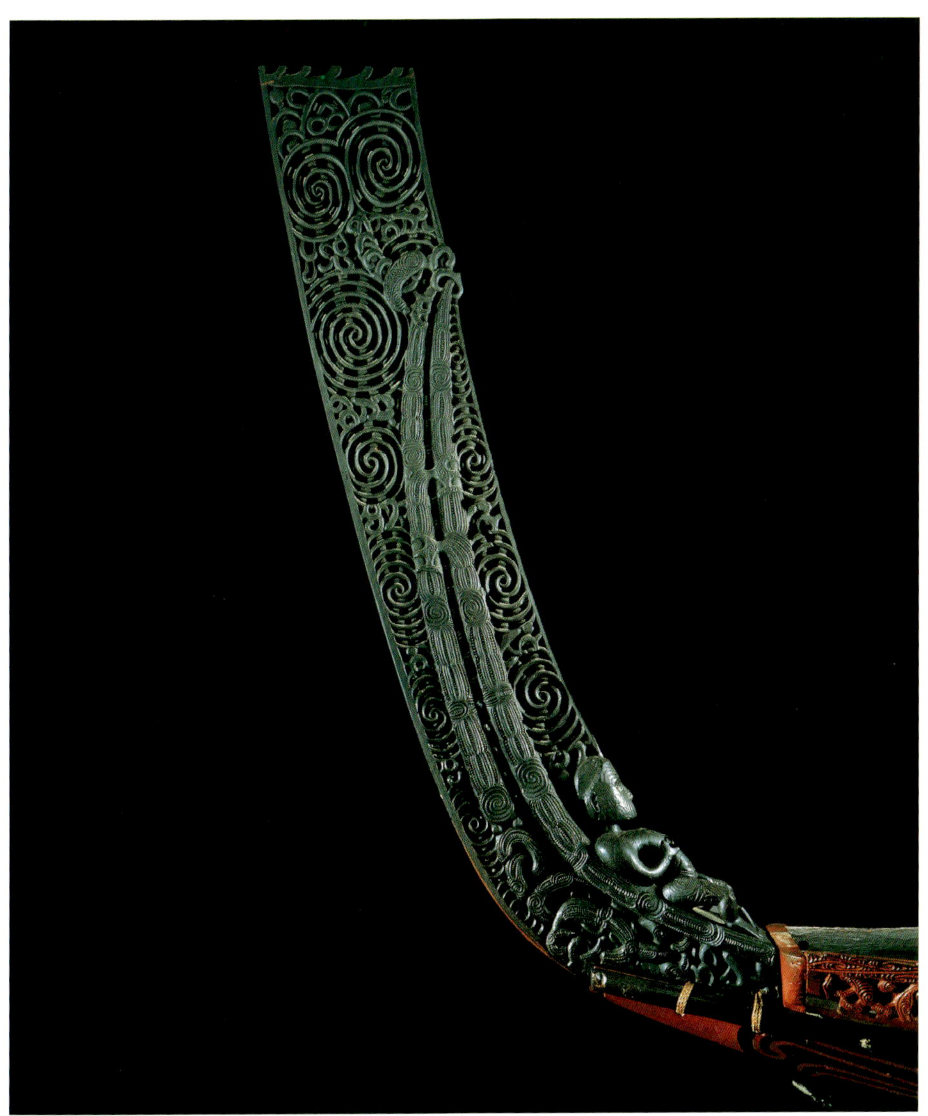

◄ 3K. haumi (canoe bow cover)
955 mm x 290 mm
wood
Puke Ariki A 82.500
on loan from Patea Historical Society

^ 3L. taurapa (canoe sternpost) of
Te Toki-a-Tapiri waka taua (war canoe)
1.83 m (h)
totara wood
carved c. 1840 by Rongowhakaata craftsmen
Auckland Museum Tamaki Paenga Hira AM 150
presented to Auckland Museum by the
New Zealand government in 1885

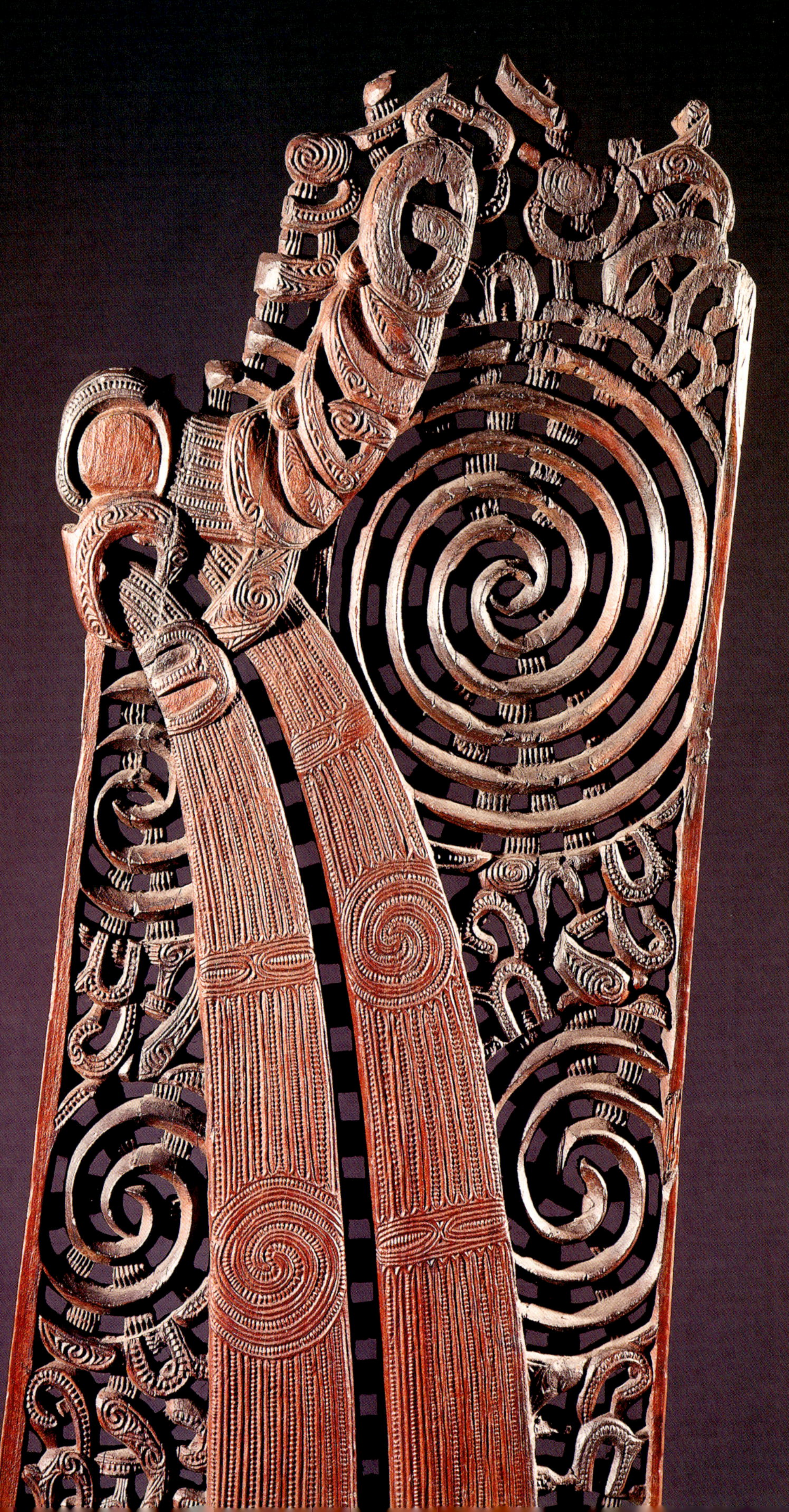

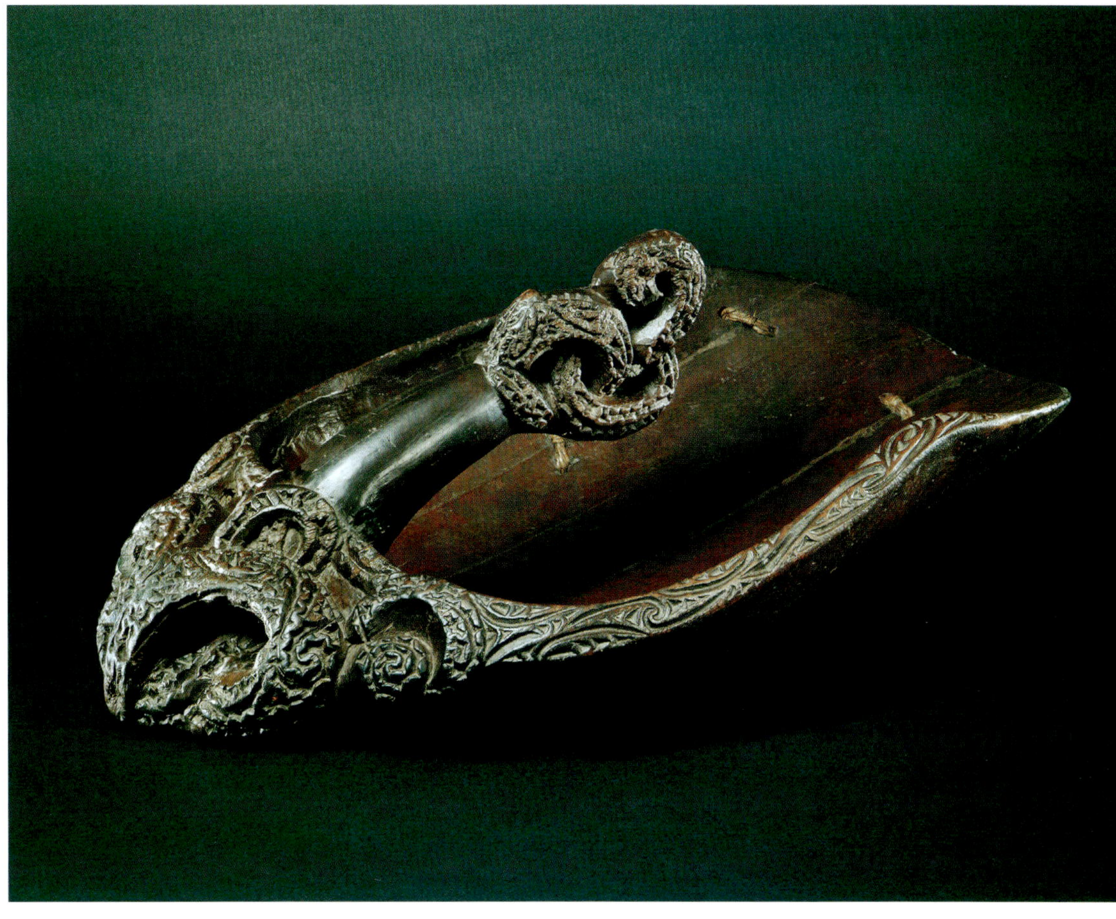

< 3M. taurapa (canoe stern post)
1.652 m
wood
carved between 1831 and 1832 at Koputuroa in Horowhenua
by Ihakara Tukumaru of the Ngati Rongo hapu (subtribe) of
Ngati Raukawa for the waka taua Te Whangawhanga Te Manawa
on loan from Canterbury Museum E 158.936

^ 3N. [23] tiheru (bailer)
457 mm
wood
Canterbury Museum E 84.10

4. TUMATAUENGA

^Tumatauenga is the only son of Ranginui and Papatuanuku who is said to have emerged undefeated from the conflicts that followed their separation. Not surprisingly, he is recognised as the god of war and therefore a figure associated with weaponry. While some narratives also describe him as an evil force, stories of Tumatauenga's battles demonstrate the significance of utu (revenge, reciprocity) in times of conflict in order to maintain social balance. Perhaps this is why — as a signifier of stability — rangatira (chiefs) owned heavily decorated 'ceremonial' weapons, and important ancestors are often depicted in wood carvings holding cleavers and staffs (pl. 4A).

Of all the thrusting cleavers, the mere pounamu (pl. 4B) was the most highly prized due to the difficulties associated with obtaining pounamu from its source on the West Coast of the South Island, and the complex shaping process of chipping and grinding. The weapon made a formidable opponent, because of its weight, when used in an attacking motion and its rigidity as a defence against attacks from staffs, such as taiaha. Other thrusting cleavers include the whalebone and wooden wahaika (pl. 4C), with its figurative embellishment and nipped edge, the double-lobed kotiate (pl. 4A), and the teardrop-shaped patu onewa, made of stone, and patu paraoa, made of whalebone. All these weapons were flat with long, often sharp, edges designed to concentrate the full force of blows made to the ribs and head in close combat. Fighters had to be agile on their feet, and a hole through the weapon's handle allowed for a wristband to ensure that the cleaver did not slip from the hand. When not in use as weapons, these cleavers were, and still are, used as gesticulation aids in whaikorero (formal oratory); when flourished with grace and skill, they signify an orator's authority and customary knowledge.

'Taiaha' is one of a number of names used to describe a hardwood weapon with a long-handled staff and a blade-like end, sometimes decorated with a dog hair and feather collar (pl. 4D). Although often described as 'spears', these weapons are never thrown but are used for striking and thrusting. The wide end of the staff is flat and acts as a cleaver, gradually rounding-out in diameter along the length of the shaft, which is a hand grip and is used as a blocking tool. The literal 'head', at the opposite end, is carved with a face on each side — a pair of eyes, usually inlaid with shell irises, carved above the collar from which emerges a tongue with a pointed edge used for jabbing. Some kaikorero also use taiaha to dramatise and underscore their speeches.

Men (and occasionally women) are still trained in the use of these weapons. The arrival of muskets, acquired from Europeans, caused a dramatic decline in hand-to-hand combat in the early nineteenth century. Although Maori weaponry manufacture was affected by this, it did not completely disappear. Weapons continued to be made for oratory and for sale to tourists. A recent revival in interest, inspired by the popularity of Asian martial arts, has created a renaissance in the art of handling weapons and the arts employed to manufacture these taonga.

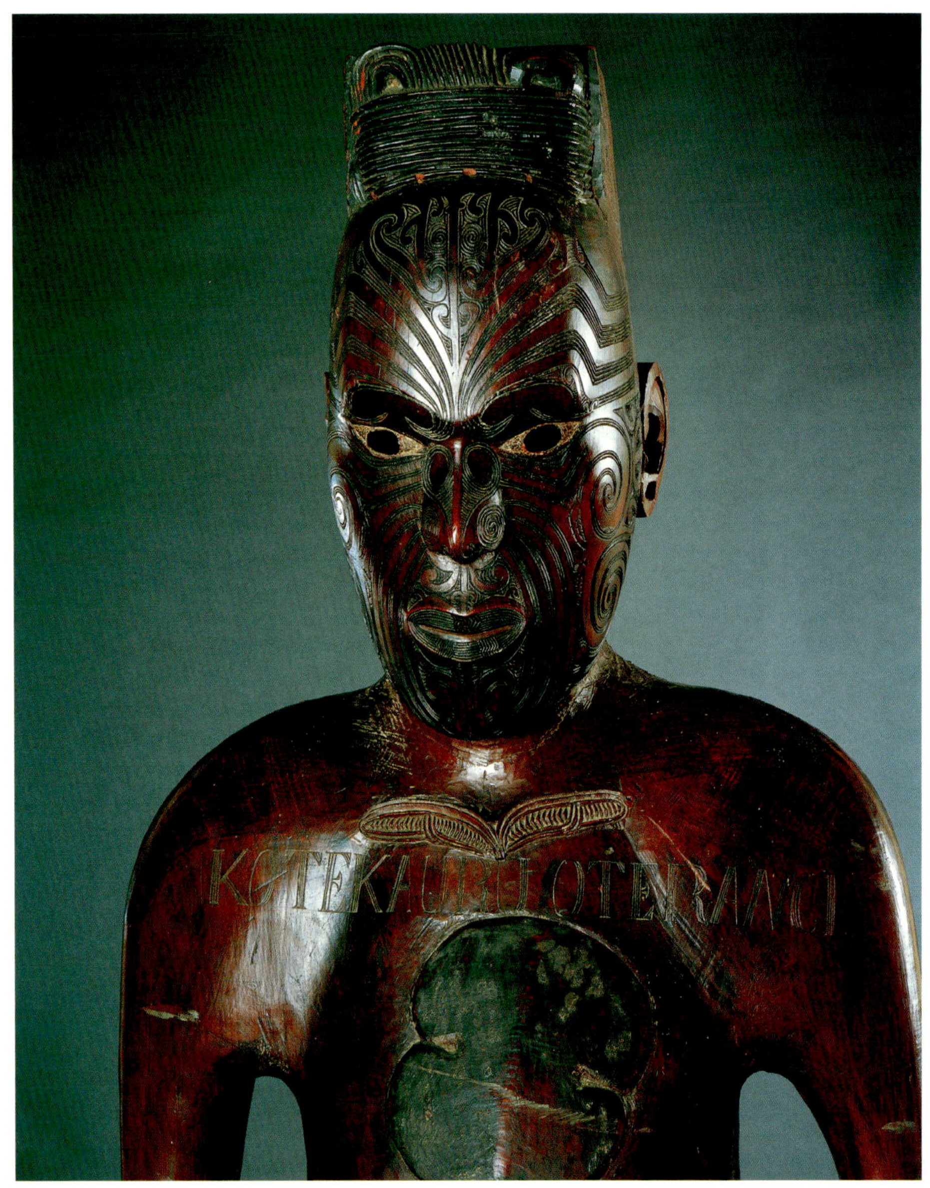

^ 4A. 'Te Kauru-o-te-rangi'
poutokomanawa (column figure)
1.44 m (h)
wood
found in Pakowhai, Napier
Hawke's Bay Museum 37/748

> 4B. 'Iwirakau' mere pounamu (cleaver)
384 mm (l) x 118 mm (w)
pounamu (greenstone, New Zealand jade)
Auckland Museum Tamaki Paenga Hira AM 505
purchased from Edward Walker

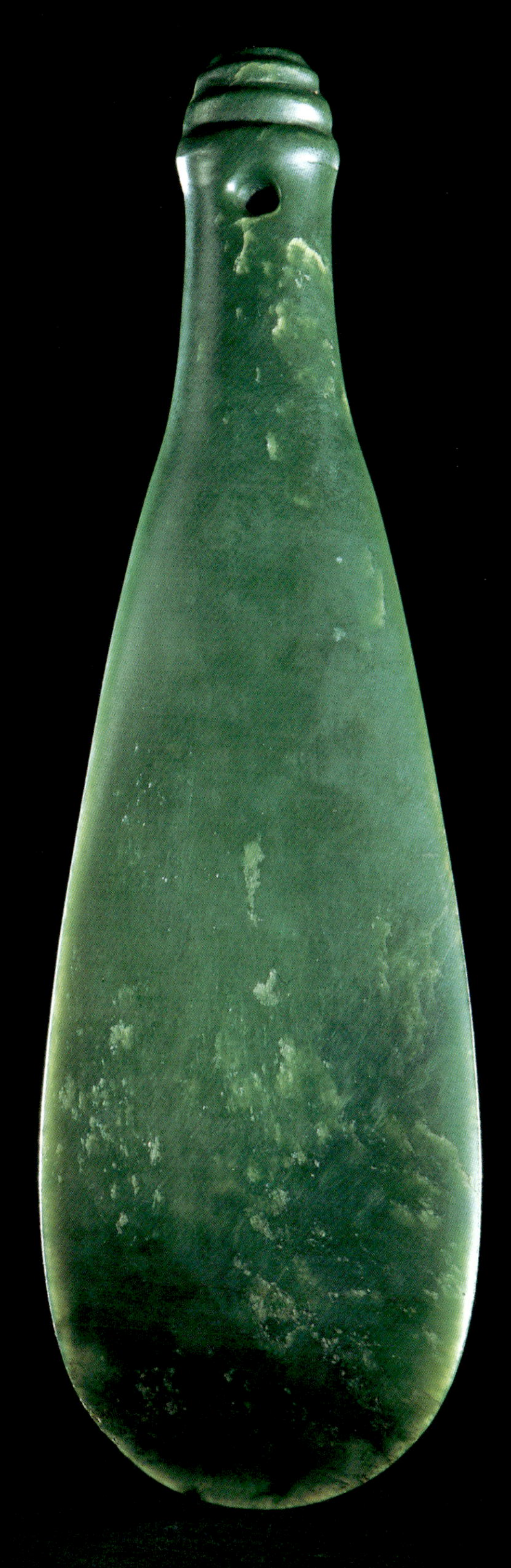

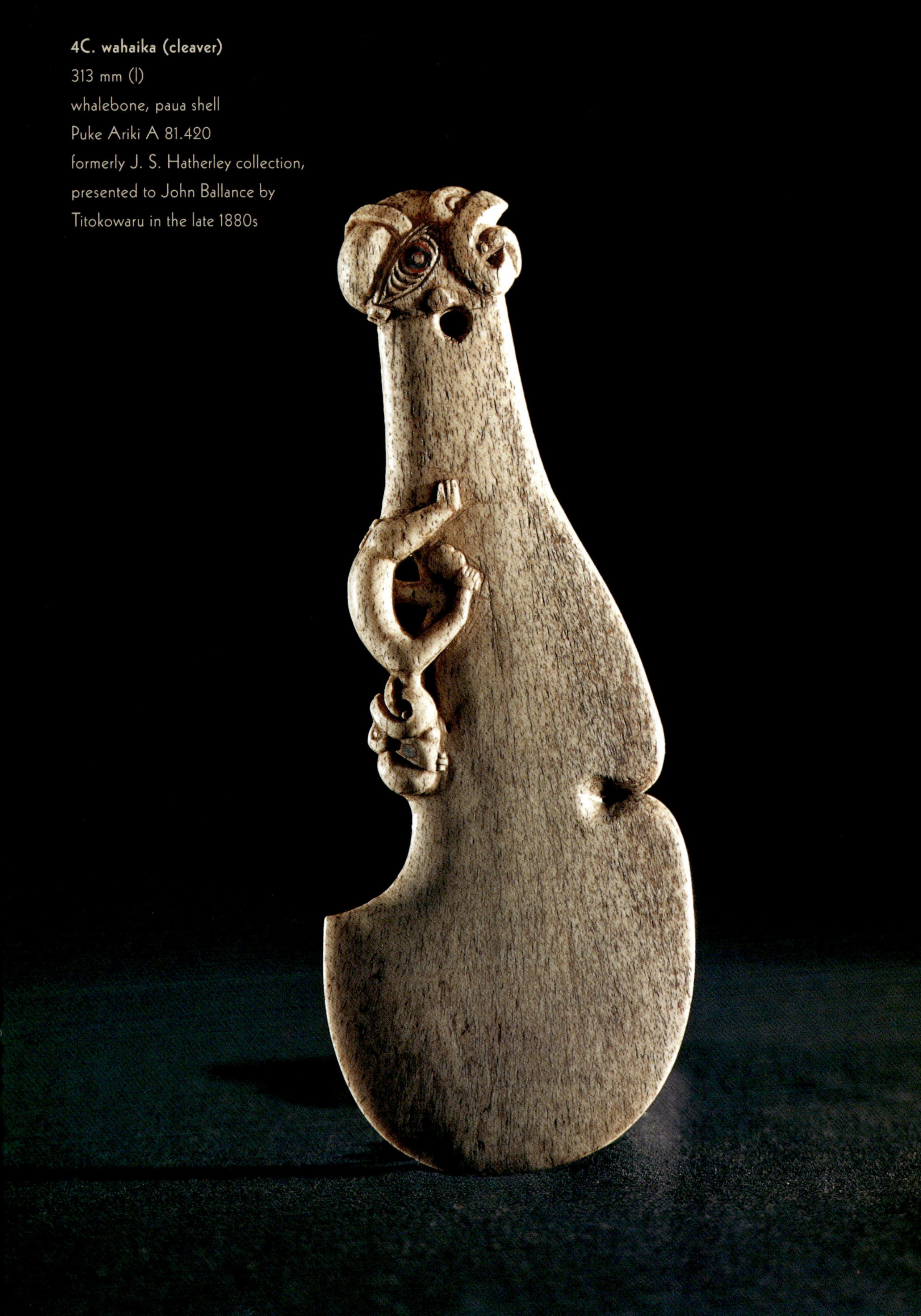

4C. wahaika (cleaver)
313 mm (l)
whalebone, paua shell
Puke Ariki A 81.420
formerly J. S. Hatherley collection,
presented to John Ballance by
Titokowaru in the late 1880s

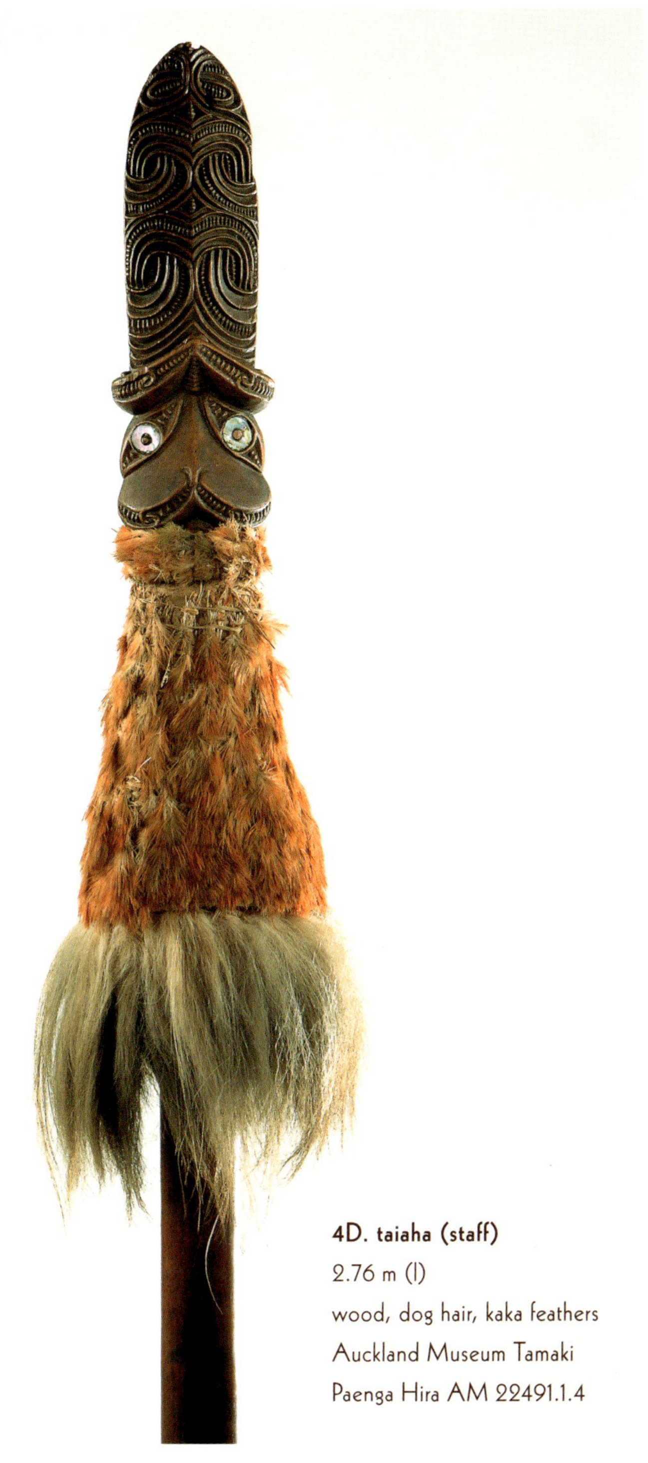

4D. taiaha (staff)
2.76 m (l)
wood, dog hair, kaka feathers
Auckland Museum Tamaki
Paenga Hira AM 22491.1.4

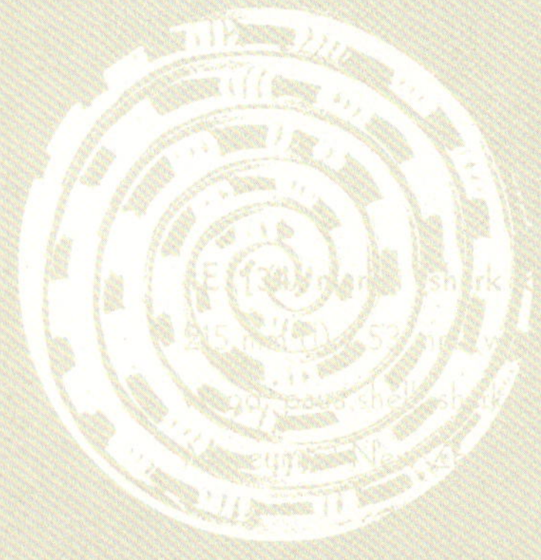

5. RONGOMATANE

Rongomatane, one of the sons of Ranginui and Papatuanuku, is a god associated with cultivated foods, fertility, peace and industry. During the conflict between his siblings, after the primeval parents were separated, his brother Tumatauenga, the god of war, developed the ko (digging stick) to harvest Rongomatane's children, including the hue (gourd, *Lagenaria vulgaris*), kumara (sweet potato, *Ipomoea batatas*) and taro (root, *Colocasia esculenta*). Through a process of cooking, these plants change from a tapu (restricted, sacred, special) to noa (free from tapu) state and are regarded as having a reduced status when compared to other elements of the Maori world. While some narratives portray him as a fierce opponent, Rongomatane is also remembered as a peace broker, although his inability to resolve the differences between his brothers set in place the continuing battle between the sea and land.

The divination of Rongomatane through the use of whakapakoko ('god sticks'; pl. 5A) was thought to aid the harvest. These were wooden sticks, around 300 mm high, bound with cord and carved with the head of a deity whose spirit resides within. By manipulating the whakapakoko and reciting karakia, tohunga (experts) were able to consult the deity. Once cultivated, food was often stored over the winter months in underground or semi-subterranean storehouses, and preserved fish and bird meat, contained in calabashes (pl. 5B), were kept in pataka, or small gabled buildings with front porches elevated on one to four poles (pls 2C & 2D). The pataka held the resources of the group, and symbolised their wealth, as recognised in the Maori proverb 'Ko te tohu o te rangatira, he pataka whakairo e tu ana i roto i te pa tuwatawata' — 'The sign of a chief is a carved storehouse standing within a palisaded pa' (Phillipps 1952: 95). Highly embellished pataka were built in some areas during the late eighteenth and early nineteenth centuries, their elaborate carvings reflecting the abundance of resources held within and the fertility and lineage of the host group. For instance, a number of central and eastern North Island pataka maihi depicted beached whales being hauled in to shore for butchery, kuwaha illustrated founding ancestors (pls 5C & 5D), while amo (front side panels) and pane (porch ridgepole) carvings showed couples locked in procreating embraces. To protect them from being seized or destroyed during the Musket Wars of the early nineteenth century, Maori sometimes dismantled and hid pataka elements in swamps and caves. During the 1820s the Whanau-a-Apanui tribe secreted the carvings of the Te Potaka pataka (pls 5E, 5F & 9C) in a cave at Te Kaha until their recovery in 1912, and they have since joined a number of museum-held pataka elements acquired through expedition, accident and tribal gift or loan.

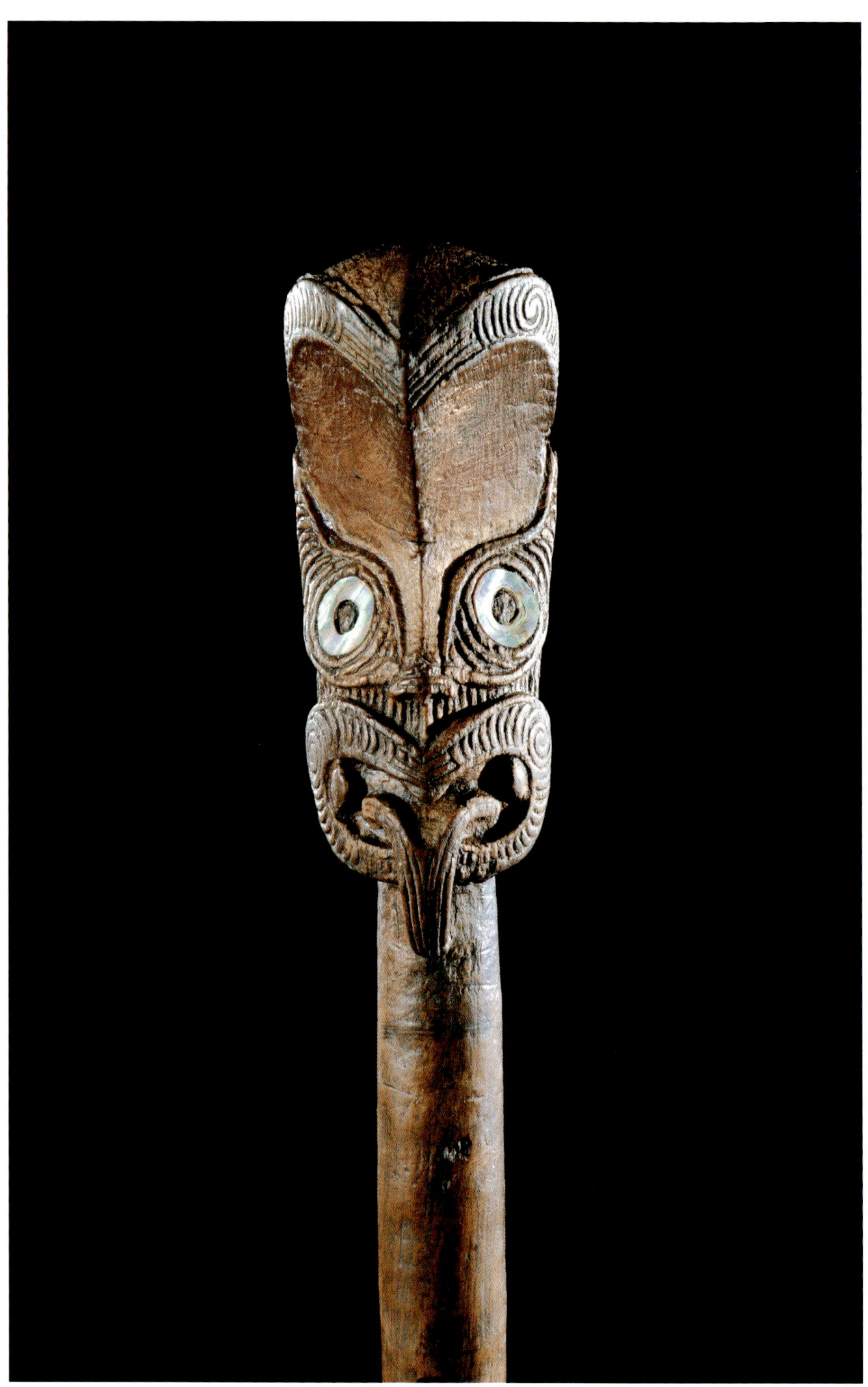

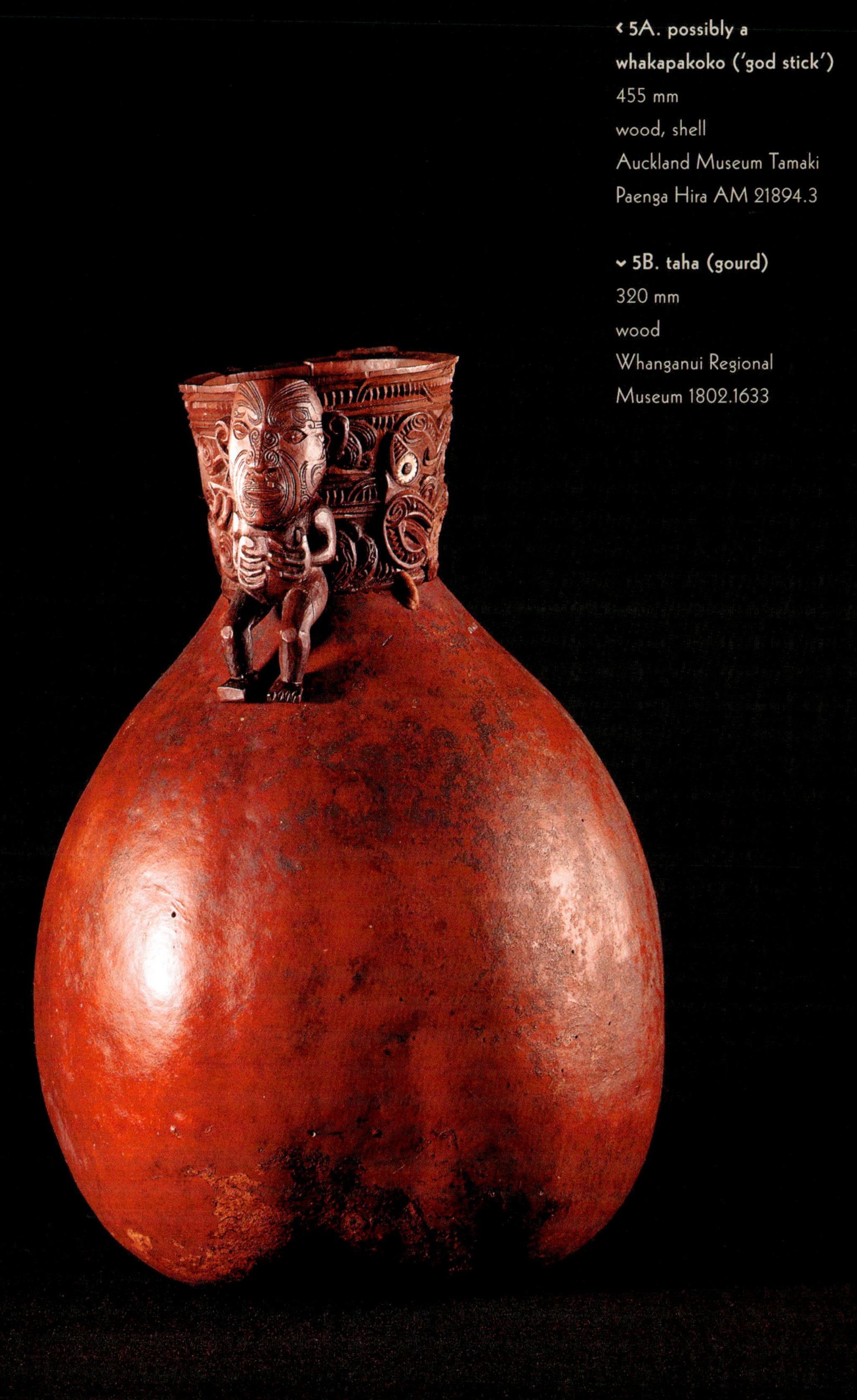

‹ 5A. possibly a
whakapakoko ('god stick')
455 mm
wood, shell
Auckland Museum Tamaki
Paenga Hira AM 21894.3

⌄ 5B. taha (gourd)
320 mm
wood
Whanganui Regional
Museum 1802.1633

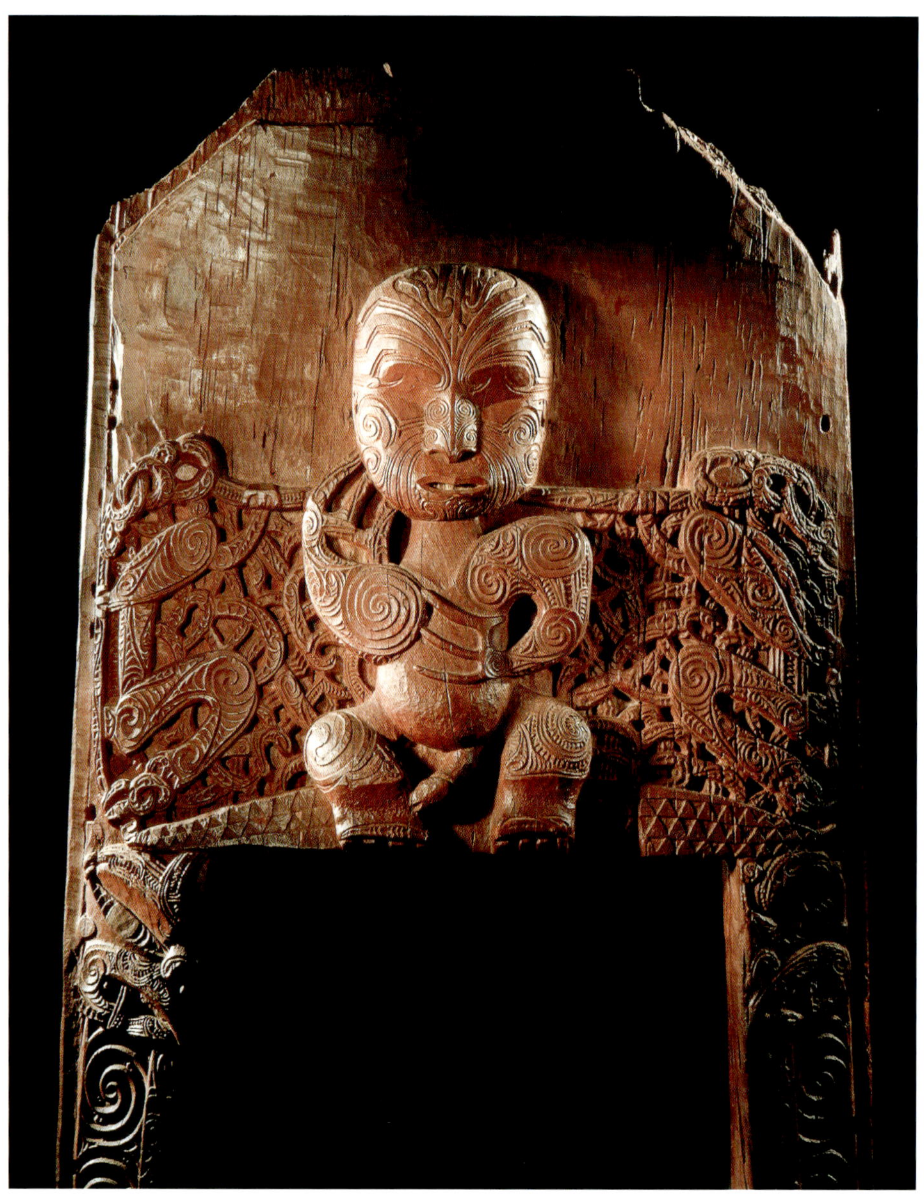

^ 5C. kuwaha pataka
(storehouse doorway)
1.155 m (h) x 655 mm (l) x 90 mm (w)
wood
from Whakatane
Auckland Museum Tamaki Paenga Hira
AM 185

› 5D. upper section of a kuwaha pataka
(storehouse doorway)
920 mm
wood
Museum of New Zealand Te Papa Tongarewa
OL 489
formerly W. O. Oldman collection, purchased
by New Zealand government in 1948

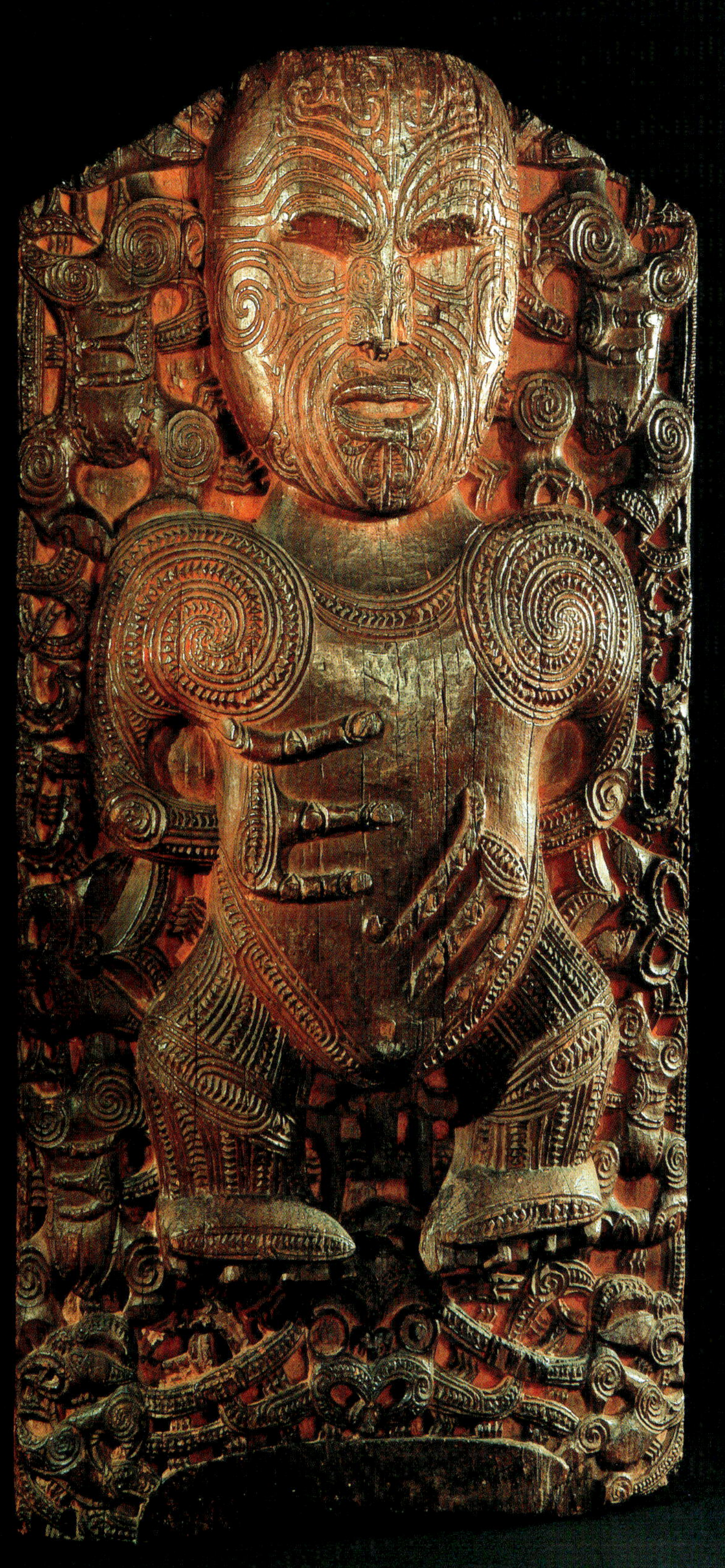

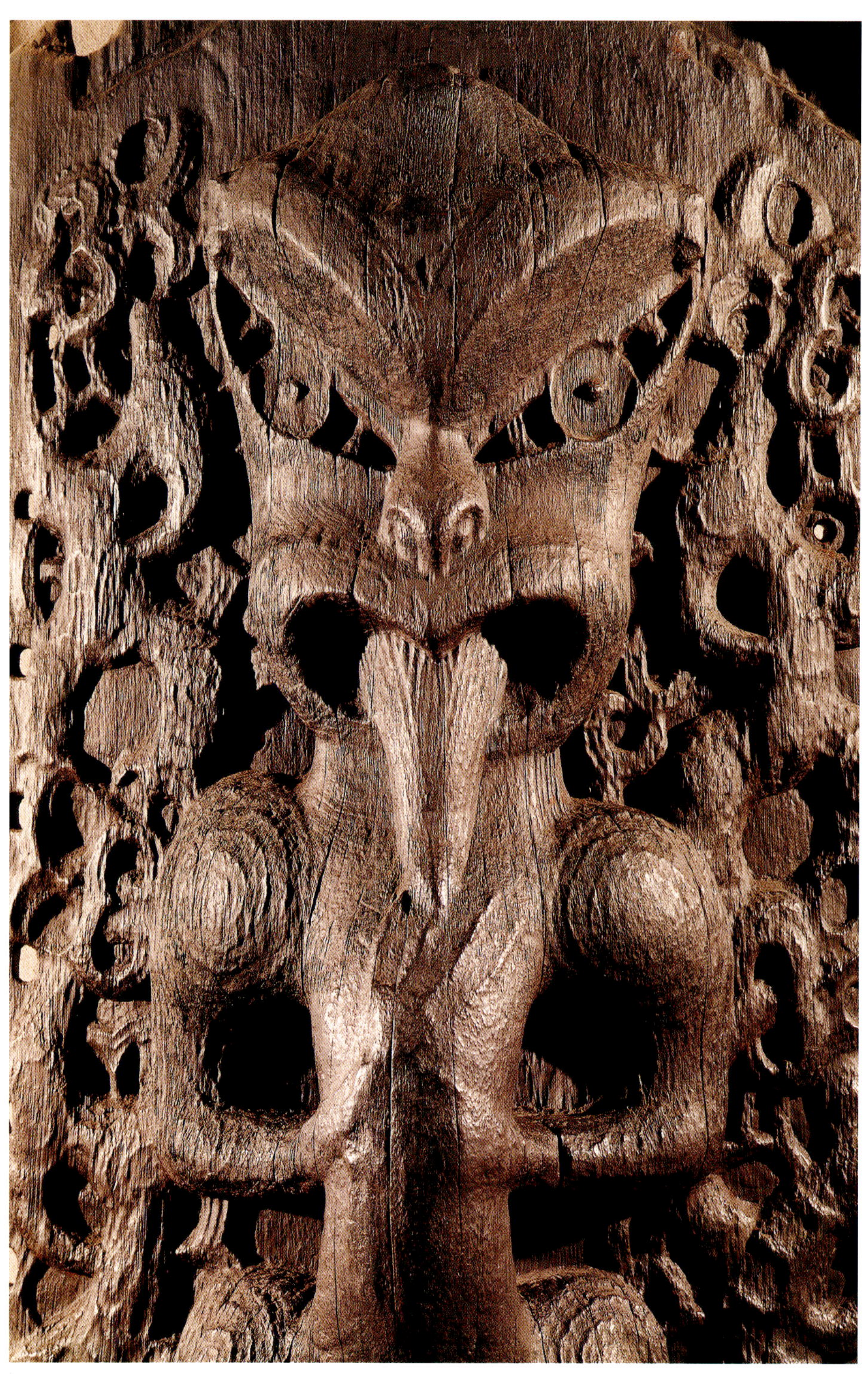

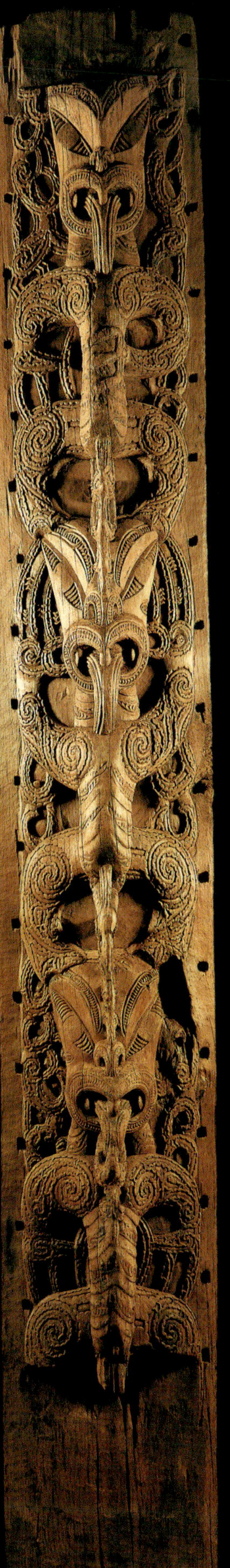

**5E & 5F. kuwaha (storehouse
doorway) and pou (panel) from
Te Potaka pataka**
totara wood
carved in the early nineteenth century
Auckland Museum Tamaki Paenga Hira
AM 22065 (kuwaha), AM 22064
(pou)
formerly Spencer collection

6. HINENUITEPO & HINETITAMA

Women feature prominently in stories about the creation of the ira tangata, or human life force, and mortality. Although Tane's relationships with female-like supernatural beings generated a number of offspring, including flora, fauna and many landscape elements of the natural world, his early liaisons, to the gods' frustration, did not produce any human women. Unable to find the female element and create a progeny that resembled the gods, Tane formed a being from the earth, usually known by the name of Hineahuone, brought her to life and then began a relationship that produced a human daughter, most often referred to as Hinetitama. With her true identity concealed from her, Hinetitama cohabitated with Tane and continued a human lineage with the birth of many daughters until she discovered that the father of her children was also her own father. Devastated, she left him for Rarohenga (the underworld) where she assumed the identity Hinenuitepo, the great woman of the dark or death. Her role is to welcome her children when they depart life. In a daring attempt to restore immortality, the legendary ancestor Mauitikitikiataranga, or Mauipotiki as he is also known, climbed into Hinenuitepo's birth canal while she was sleeping, to seize her heart, but was instead crushed to death between her thighs when she was woken by a fantail unable to contain its laughter at the sight unfolding. Fertility, procreation and human abundance are significant themes in these narratives, particularly when they are associated with the concept of women as the vessels of life and death.

Waka are vessels associated with containment and travel, and while the term encompasses a wide variety of water-borne vessels, it can also be applied to containers for the bones of the dead, commonly known as waka tupapaku or waka koiwi, and containers for precious goods, called waka huia. In Northland, the remains of highly ranked people were left to decay in prohibited areas; their bones were later recovered as part of the hahu or hahunga ceremony and placed in a figurative waka tupapaku stood upright inside caves (pls 6A, 6B & 6C). A small figure depicted beneath the main character, on one waka tupapaku (pl. 6D) may represent children emerging from, and Mauitikitikiataranga climbing into, Hine, in both her roles as Hinetitama and Hinenuitepo. In this instance her body is represented as the portal between the mortal world and Hawaiki. With the arrival of the missions and Christianity, Maori began to adopt the Western practice of interment, and hahunga and waka tupapaku carving declined as a consequence. However, the Northland figurative style was revived in the mid 1930s by the School of Maori Arts and Crafts in Rotorua, which used as models a number of waka tupapaku from the Hokianga district that had been recovered by collectors and sold to Auckland Museum.

Waka huia contained prized possessions. As they were sometimes suspended by cords from whare (house) ceilings, all their surfaces including the base were elaborately carved (see boxes illustrated, pls 6E, 6F, 6G & 6H). Once Maori adopted European-style tables and shelves, decoration was confined to the sides and tops. One striking feature of early waka huia, particularly the papahou rectangular type, is the profusion of figures, sometimes obviously male or female and occasionally in the process of procreation, which cover their surfaces. This depiction of human abundance and fertility can be contrasted with that displayed by the waka tupapaku, which are usually single figures, predominantly female (see pl. 6D) but occasionally male (pl. 6A) or genderless (pls 6B & 6C), with mouths seemingly contorted from taking the last breath of life. The figures of these waka exist at life's edge.

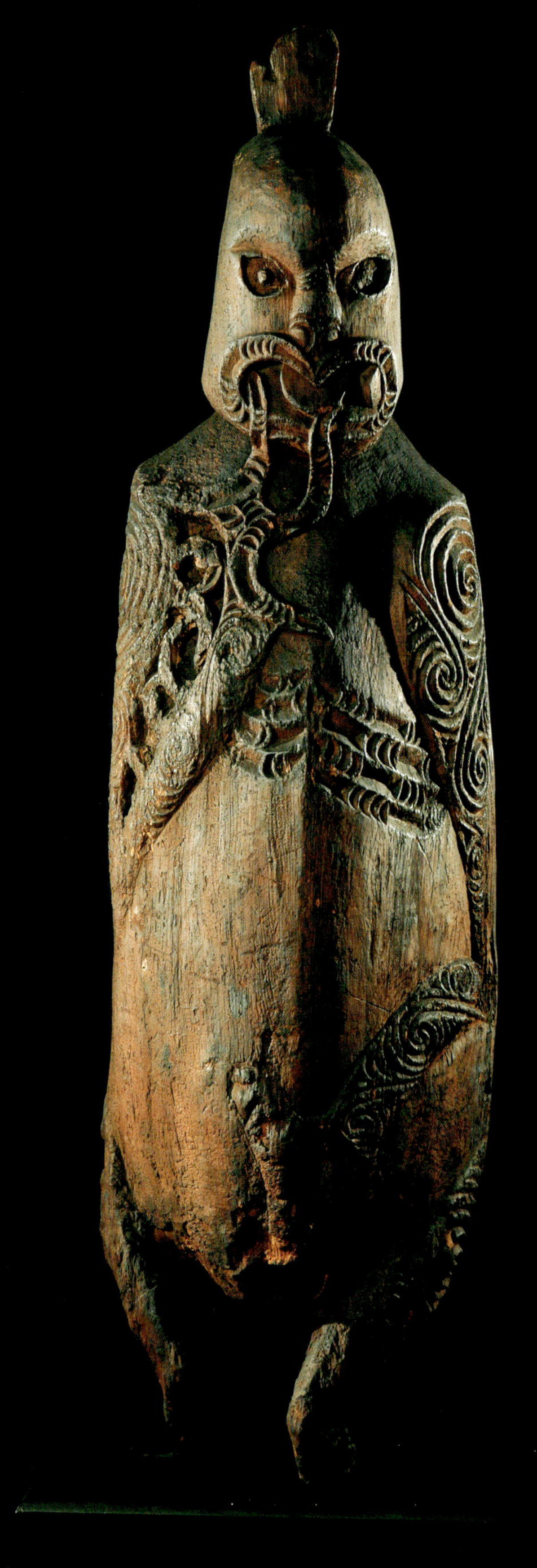

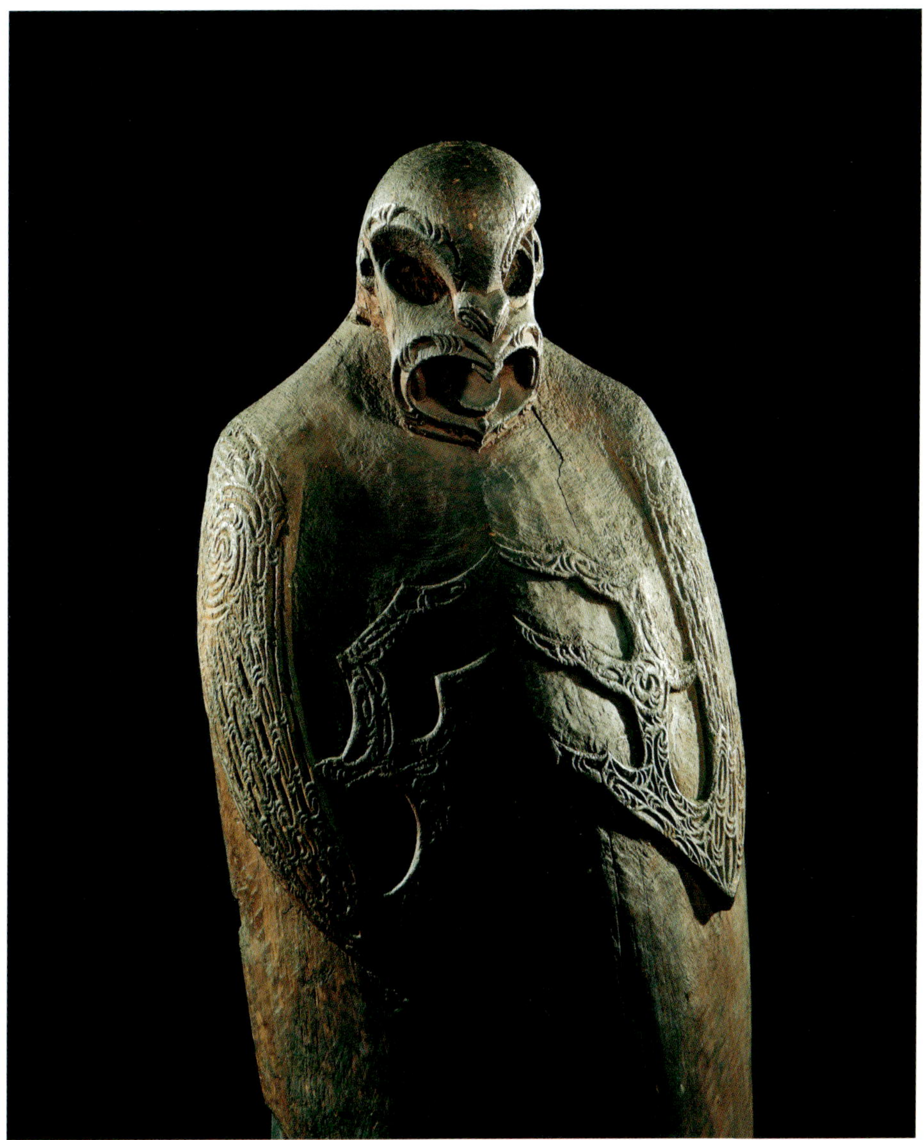

‹ 6A. waka tupapaku (bone casket)
1.2 m (h)
wood
no details of recovery location
Museum of New Zealand Te Papa
Tongarewa ME 2660
presented by A. H. Turnbull in 1913

⌃ 6B. waka tupapaku (bone casket)
980 mm (h)
wood
no details of recovery location
Museum of New Zealand Te Papa
Tongarewa ME 2659
presented by A. H. Turnbull in 1913

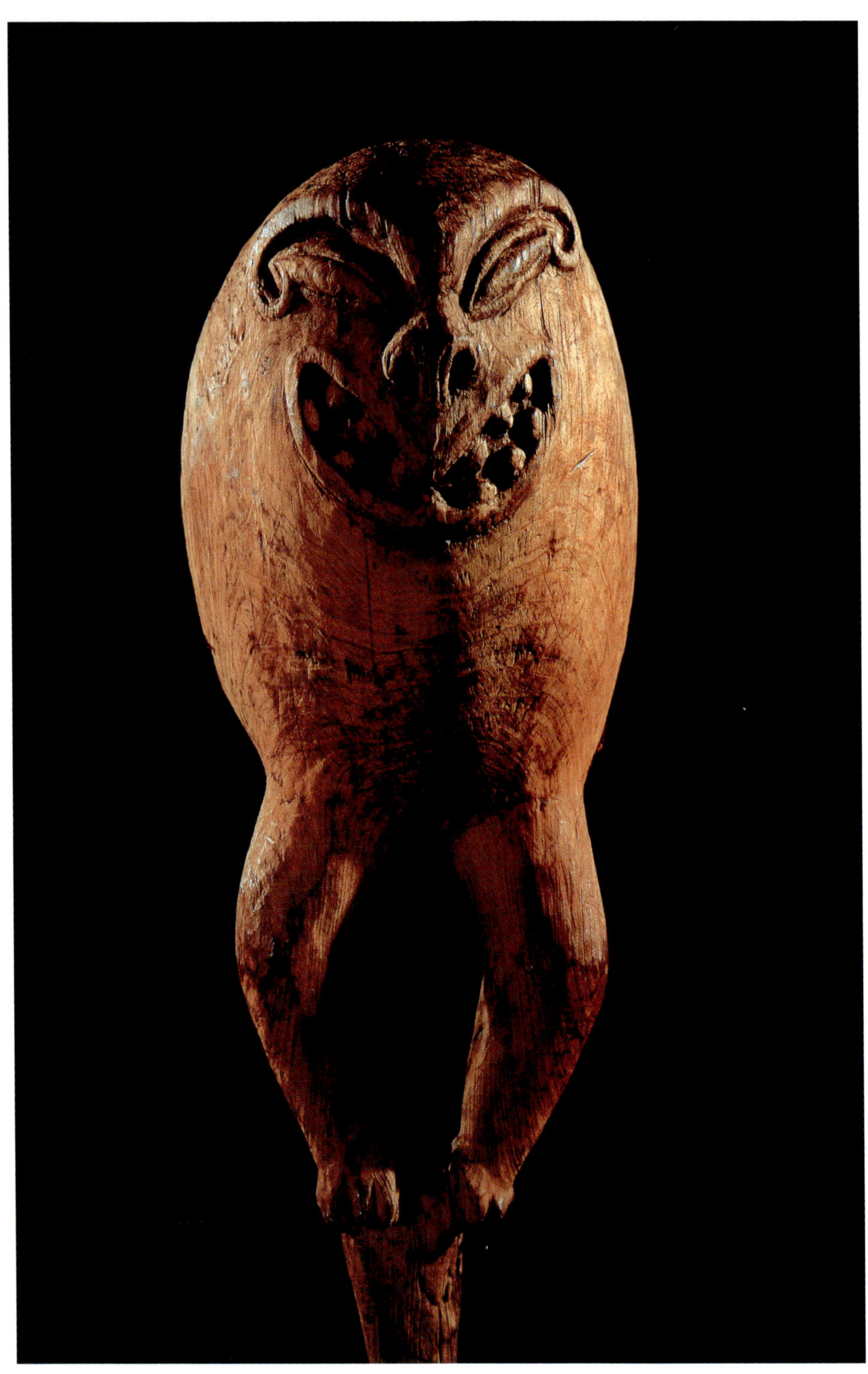

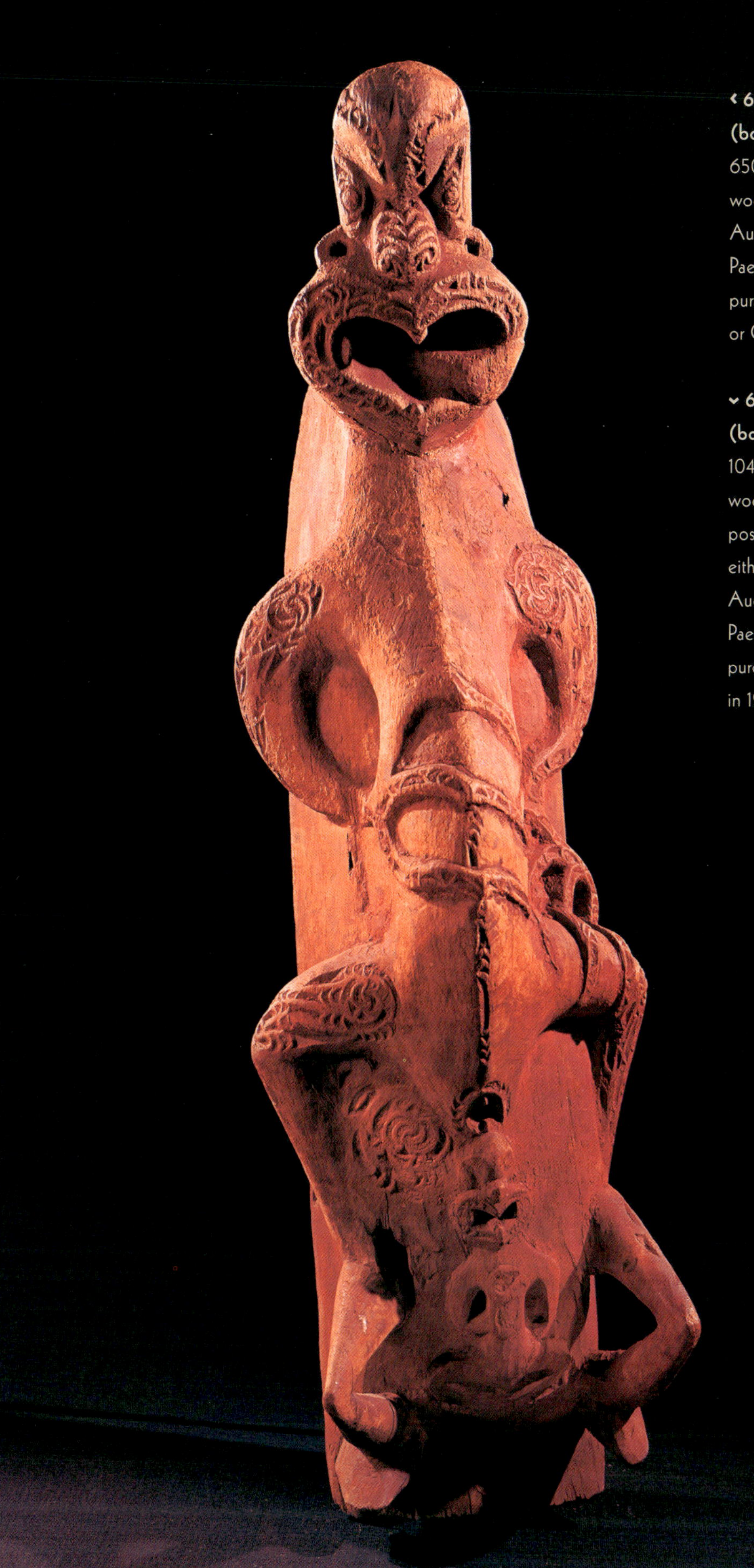

‹ 6C. waka tupapaku
(bone casket)
650 mm (h) x 220 mm (dia)
wood
Auckland Museum Tamaki
Paenga Hira AM 19458
purchased from Miss Cardno
or Cardins in 1927

⌄ 6D. waka tupapaku
(bone casket)
104 mm (h)
wood
possibly found in a cave at
either Waiomio or Kawakawa
Auckland Museum Tamaki
Paenga Hira AM 5660
purchased from Mr E. Spencer
in 1913 or 1918

6E. waka huia (treasure box)
420 mm (l) 103 mm (w) 100 mm (h)
wood, paua shell
Auckland Museum Tamaki Paenga Hira AM 31512
formerly W. O. Oldman collection OL 328

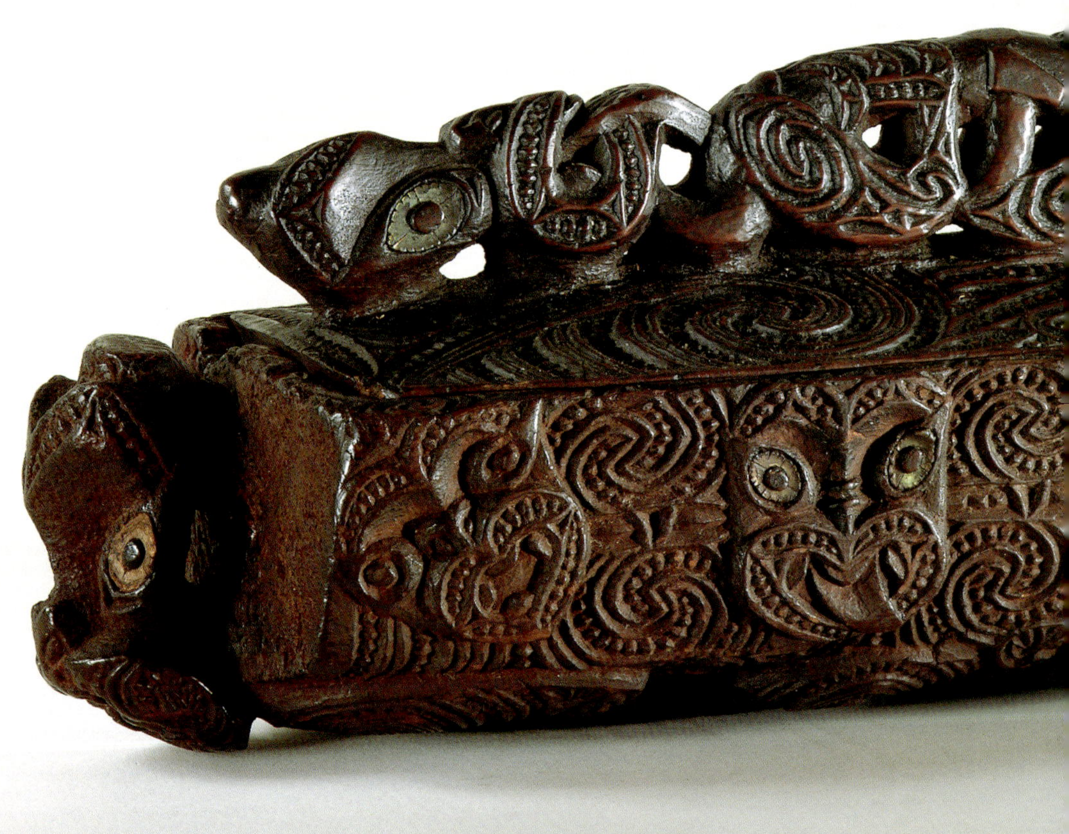

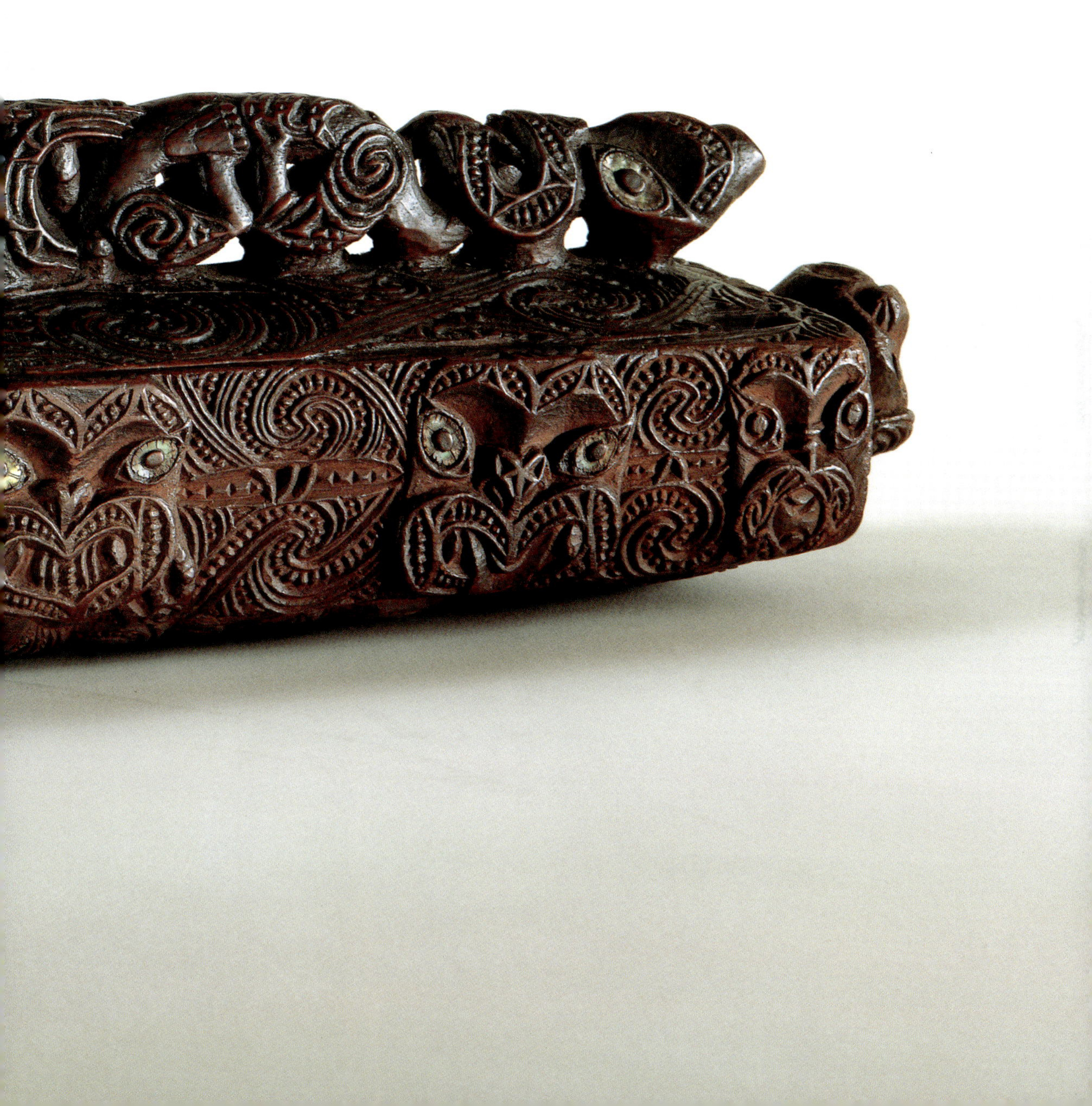

6F. papahou (treasure box)
531 mm (l)
wood
Museum of New Zealand Te Papa Tongarewa OL 331
formerly W. O. Oldman collection, purchased by
New Zealand government in 1948

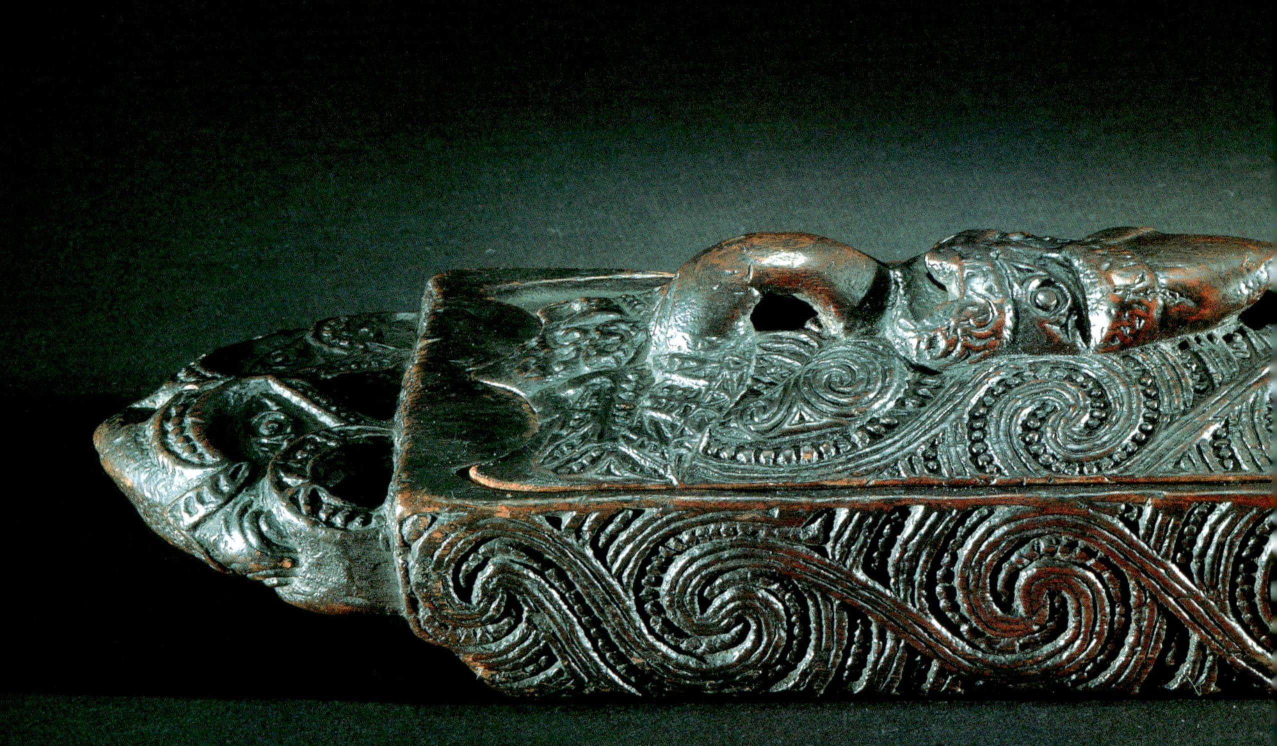

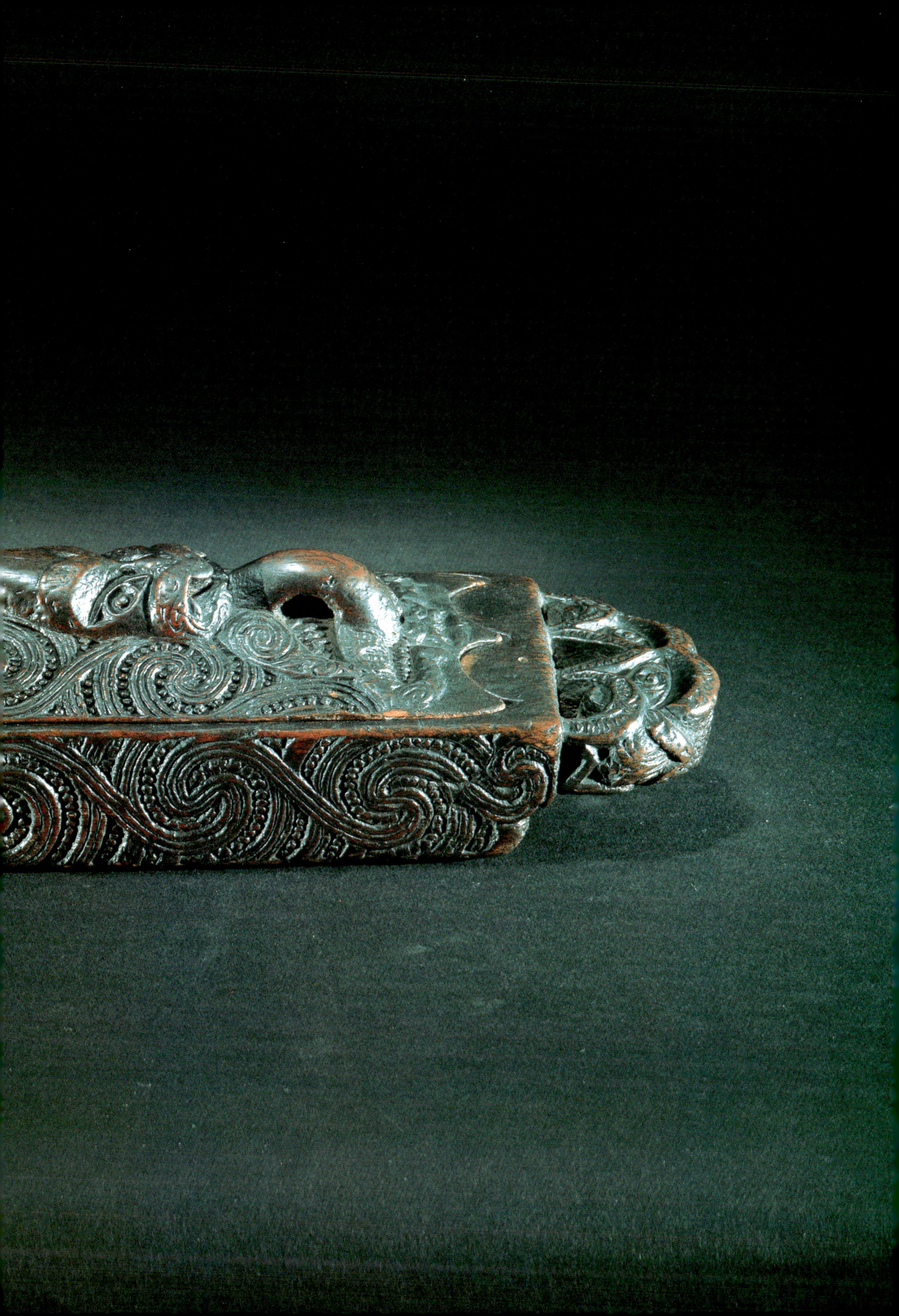

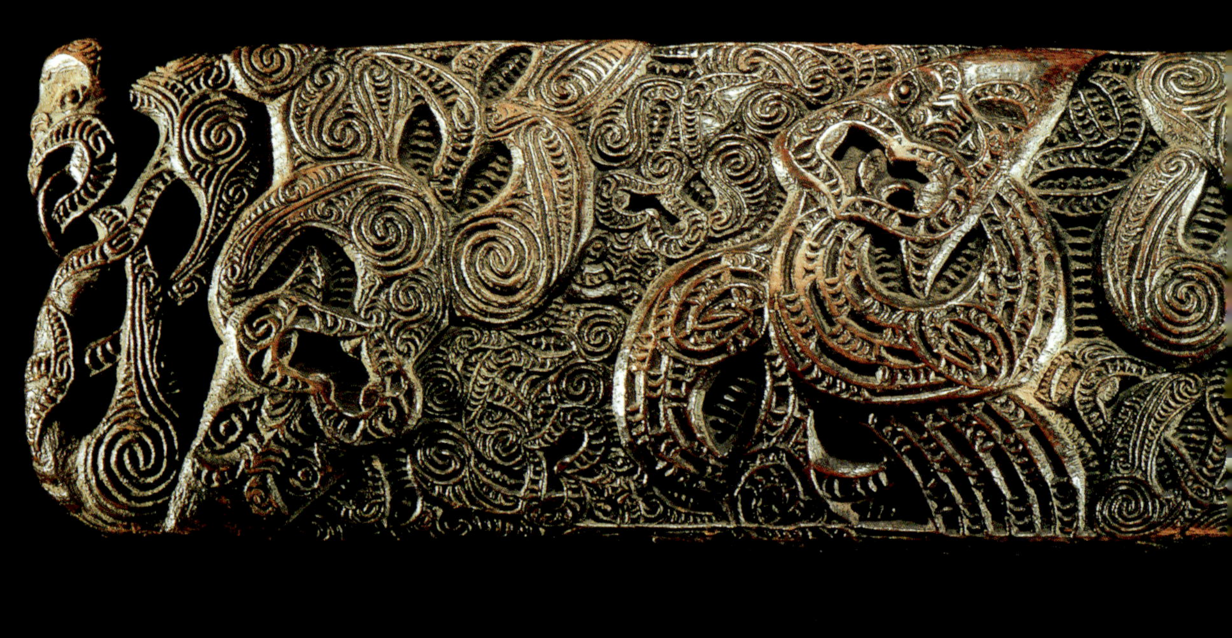

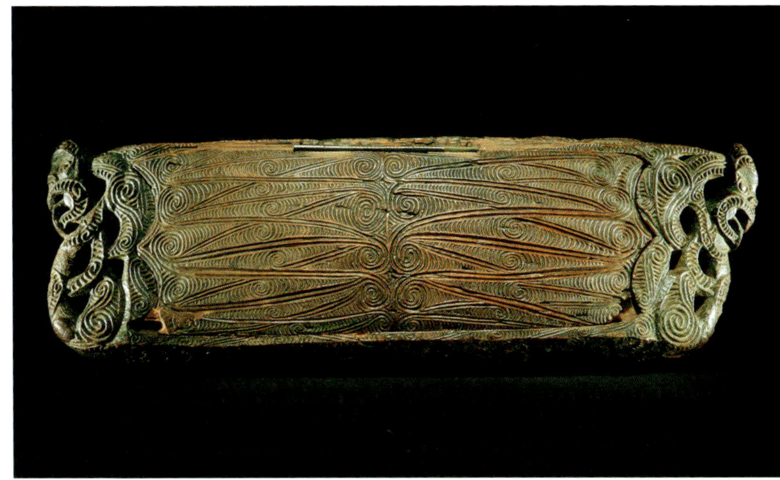

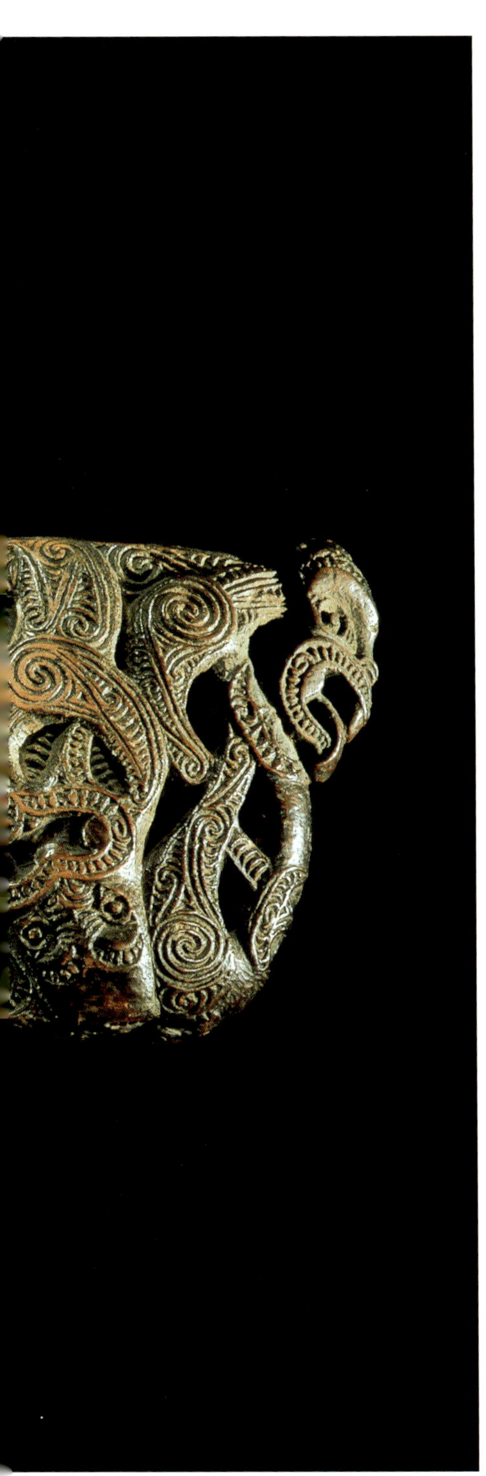

6G & 6H. top and base of a papahou (treasure box)

430 mm (l)

wood

Museum of New Zealand Te Papa Tongarewa OL 484

formerly W. O. Oldman collection, purchased by New Zealand

government in 1948

7. MATAORA

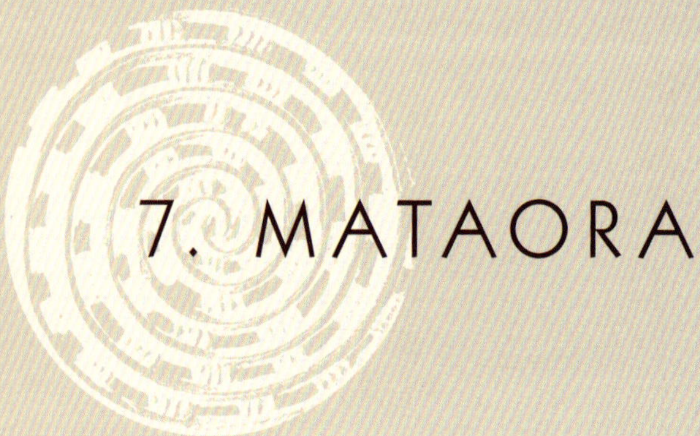

According to some tribal ancestral narratives, the mythological figure Mataora brought ta moko, and the practice of Maori tattoo, to the mortal world. His journey of discovery began when he followed his wife, Niwareka, a former inhabitant of Rarohenga, back to the underworld after she had left him. At that time in the mortal world, faces were painted rather than incised, and Mataora was surprised to see Niwareka's father, Uetonga, carving another man's face. Impressed by the beauty and permanence of the result he persuaded Uetonga to perform ta moko on him and, on returning to the mortal world, he practised and taught the art to others.

Moko is more than a body adornment, it symbolises a person's identity as an individual and as a member of a wider whanau (extended family) and iwi (tribal group). Each design illustrates elements both personal to the wearer and shared among their near and distant relatives. The practice is tapu and subject to many restrictions. People receiving ta moko are not permitted to make skin contact with food, which, as a noa entity, would result in potentially disastrous consequences for themselves and the practitioner. In customary times, the recipient of ta moko received their food through a korere, or feeding funnel (pl. 7A), with elaborate surfaces carved with the faces and often bodies of ancestors, as befitted the ritual circumstances in which these taonga were used. The tohunga's tools and implements are similarly held in high regard, as can been seen by the ipu wai ngarahu (pl. 7B) (small pigment pot) with its complexly decorated surfaces featuring faces and bodies as well as intricate patterns.

Women of suitable rank or accomplishment might receive moko to their lips, chin and forehead, shown by the illustrated female poutokomanawa (freestanding house column) figure (pl. 7C), as well as the neck, arms, breasts, lower abdomen, buttocks, thighs, hips and genital area. Men receive moko on their full faces, visible on the head of a North Auckland figure (pl. 7D), lower back, buttocks and thighs. According to Ngahuia Te Awekotuku, 'the full-facial moko of the Maori male, balanced by the complex patterning between lower back and knees, were designed and presented to inspire fear, excite admiration and arouse erotic interest' (Te Awekotuku in Blackley 1997: 111).

Moko are customarily worn as a right of inheritance, or earned through a deed of courage, and more recently have become a sign that the wearer is an accomplished cultural practitioner. Declining in popularity among males in the mid-nineteenth century, due to the fashion of beards and association with conflict and non-Western customs, ta moko survived at a low level for most of the twentieth century as a female-borne art among tourist guides and women living in isolated Maori communities. Its revival for men and women over the past thirty years has seen ta moko transformed from an art of identity, within a group, to a specifically Maori art of identity, within a wider social and global context.

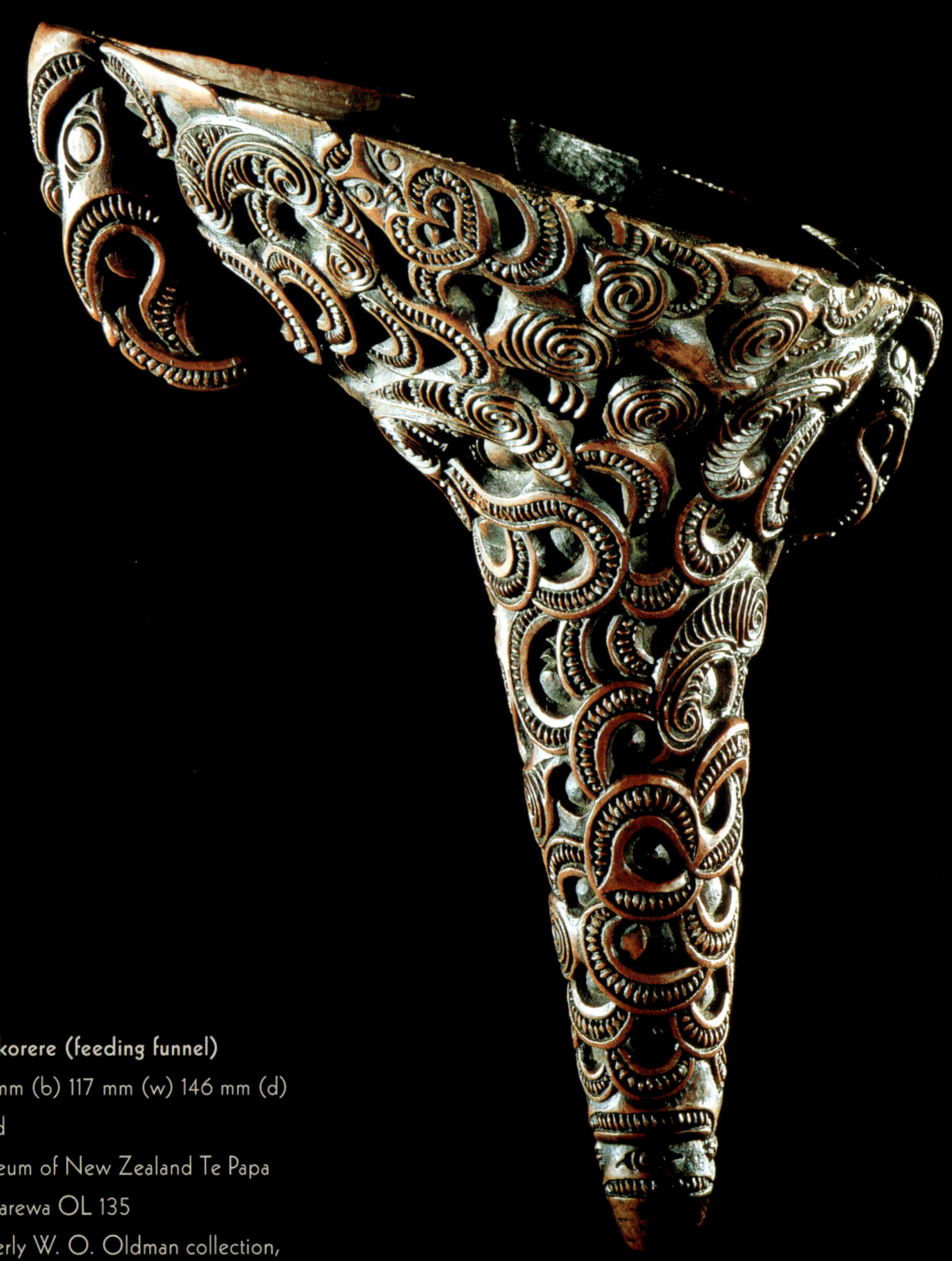

7A. korere (feeding funnel)
160 mm (b) 117 mm (w) 146 mm (d)
wood
Museum of New Zealand Te Papa
Tongarewa OL 135
formerly W. O. Oldman collection,
purchased by the New Zealand
government in 1948

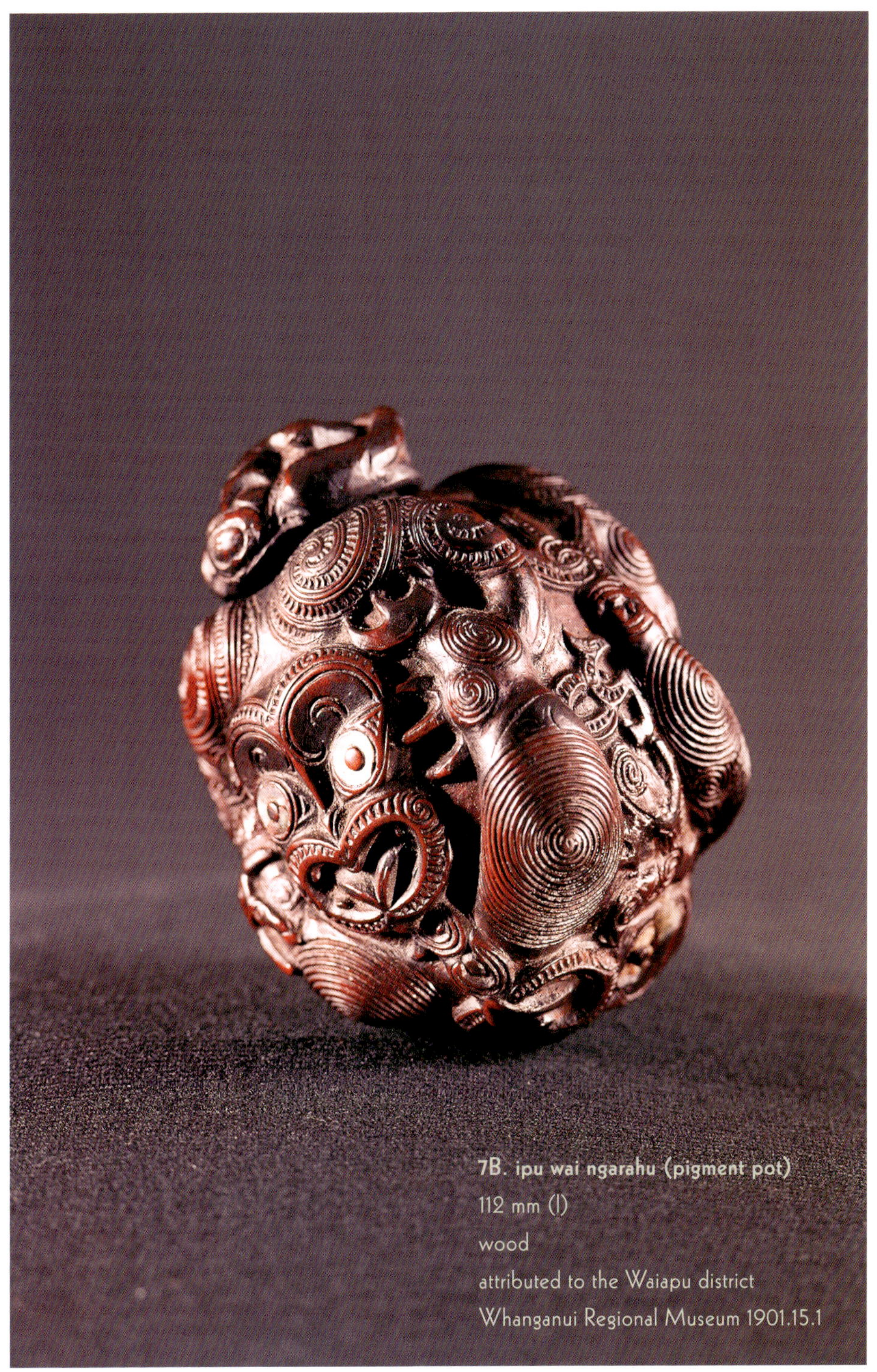

7B. ipu wai ngarahu (pigment pot)
112 mm (l)
wood
attributed to the Waiapu district
Whanganui Regional Museum 1901.15.1

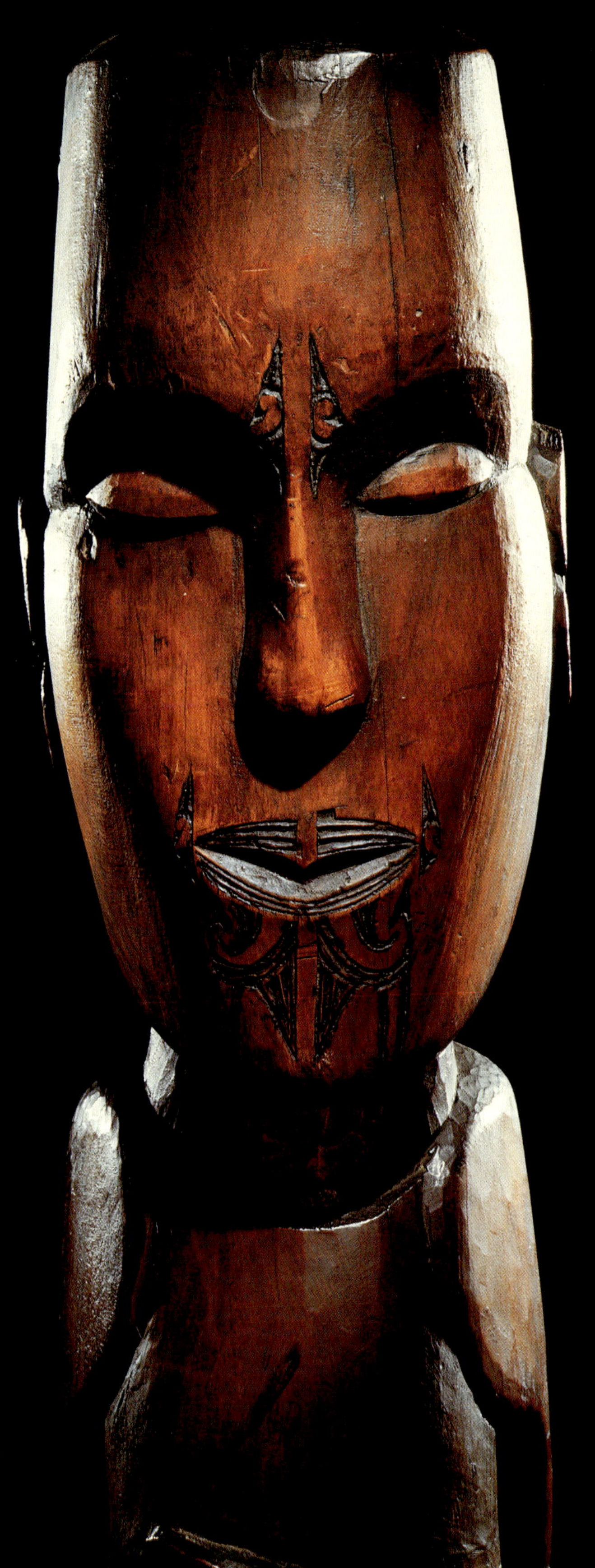

7C. poutokomanawa (interior
support post figure)
810 mm (h)
wood
from a whare near Taupo
Otago Museum D10.285
formerly Hocken collection

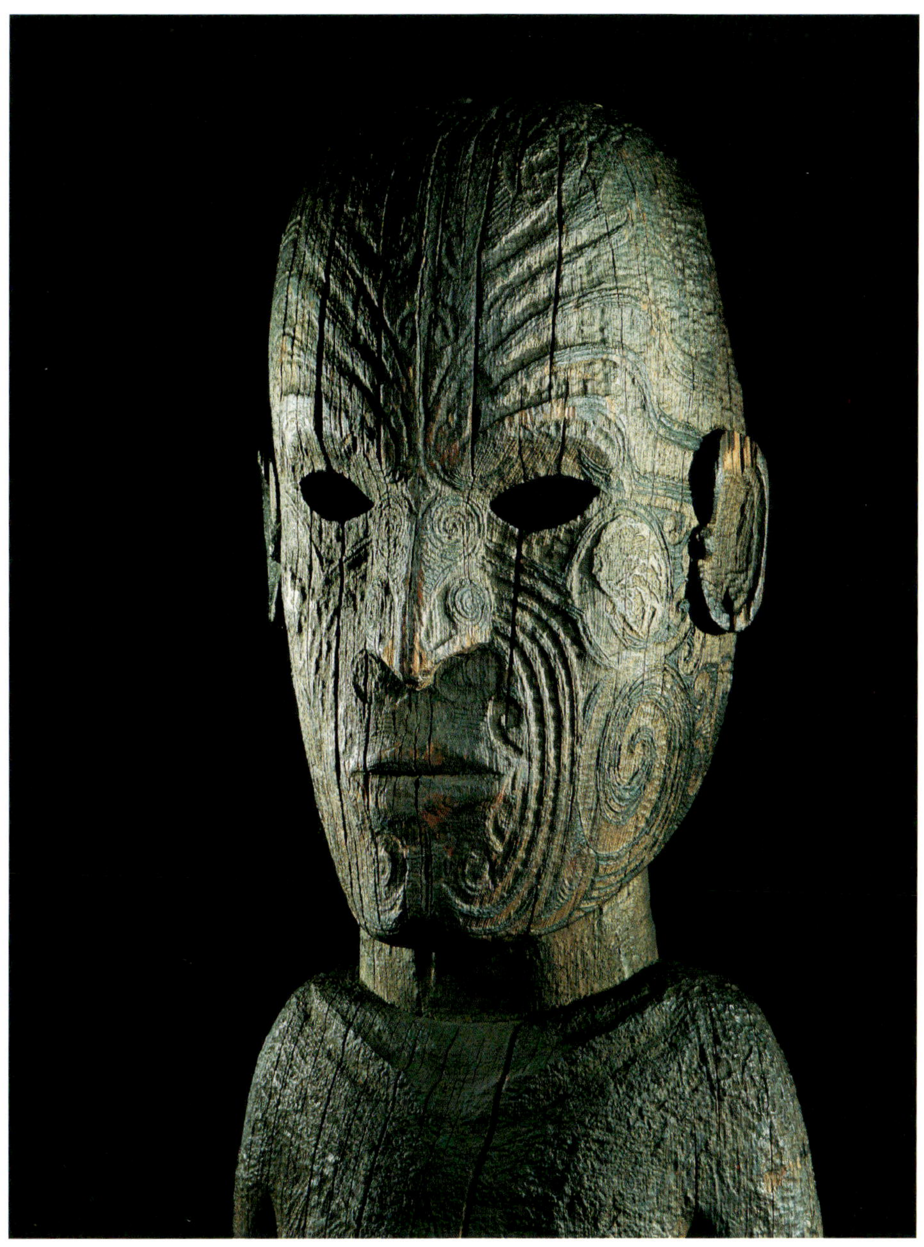

7D. figure, possibly from a palisade post
990 mm x 240 mm x 200 mm
wood
Auckland Museum Tamaki Paenga Hira AM 22737
formerly F. O. Peat collection

8. NIWAREKA

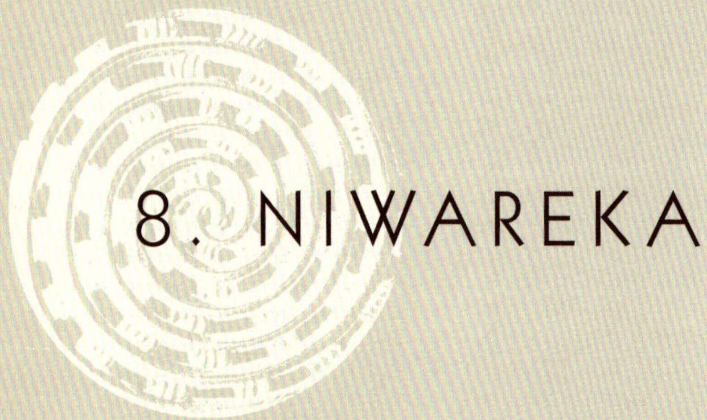

Niwareka is credited in some tribal narratives for bringing the practice of fibre art from Rarohenga to the mortal world. She is descended from supernatural underworld beings, including Hinenuitepo, but chose to cohabitate with a mortal, Mataora, until the day he struck her, and she fled back to Rarohenga. While there she made a cloak called Te Raupapanui for her father, Uetonga. She had access to woven mats, which she laid out for Mataora when she heard that he had undergone a moko kanohi after following her to the underworld. Niwareka recognised her husband by the clothing she had made for him. When the couple decided to return to the mortal world, Uetonga presented Mataora with another of her cloaks, Te Rangihaupapa, and also a belt called Te Rurukuoterangi. These garments attracted much interest on the couple's return and became the mastercopies used by mortal women.

Customary Maori clothing consists of waist mats and cloaks, made by whatu (fine twining), and belts and sandals that, like mats and sails, were created through a process of plaiting. Fibre for these processes is harvested from some varieties of harakeke (New Zealand flax, *Phormium tenax*) as well as cabbage tree leaves, sedges and climbing plants. Plaited work is prepared using the green shafts of leaves divided into strips. The dried and softened sinews of harakeke, known as muka, are rolled into cords and used in the manufacture of twined garments that could take months or years to manufacture depending on the techniques employed. To make a twined garment using customary techniques, a support frame was made by placing two turuturu whatu (garment pegs; pl. 8A) into the ground. A framework of all the vertical fibres, or whenu (warps), was suspended from a main horizontal line strung between the turuturu, and horizontal aho (wefts) were woven between them.

Different types of cloaks have become popular, as Maori clothing fashions have changed. Most Maori cloaks comprise of a 'kaupapa' foundation garment, made between the turuturu, which is either loosely or compactly twined depending on the desired quality of the completed result. Kaitaka cloaks (pl. 8B) found favour amongst the highly born of the early nineteenth century. They are tightly twined and left unadorned, apart from geometrically patterned taniko borders on their bottom and side edges, and the fineness of the garment is judged on the competency of the fibre work. Other cloaks have fibre, feather or dog hair additions secured into their kaupapa. The korowai (pl. 8C) rose to prominence in the 1830s, and is a thickly twined garment adorned with double- and triple-ply muka tags that hang and move with the wearer. With the adoption of European trends, woollen coloured squares and pompoms were sometimes added to the korowai, and in the late eighteenth and early nineteenth centuries their plain surfaces were occasionally dyed red, a colour from the Creation story associated with tapu, using kokowai (ochre). As time progressed, korowai design was standardised and the kaupapa was often left in its natural white state with black tags. Towards the end of the nineteenth century the kahu huruhuru (feather cloak; pl. 8D), made by adding a dense layer of feathers to a kaupapa, joined the korowai as another prestige garment. By this stage, Maori cloaks were only being worn over European-style clothes on ceremonial occasions, and the art of cloak making entered a period of decline due to a lack of commissions. Since the 1950s it has enjoyed a popular revival, begun under the leadership of Dame Rangimarie Hetet, and all types of cloaks are currently being manufactured by a new generation of female fibre artists, following the example of Hetet and ultimately Niwareka.

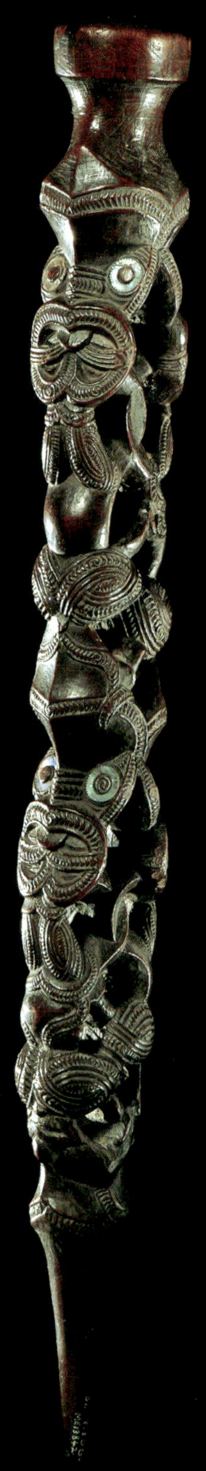

8A. turuturu whatu (garment peg)
490 mm (l) x 45 mm (w) x 56 mm (d)
wood, paua shell
Museum of New Zealand Te Papa
Tongarewa ME 13842
formerly the Tau Fletcher collection,
purchased by the museum at auction
in 1977

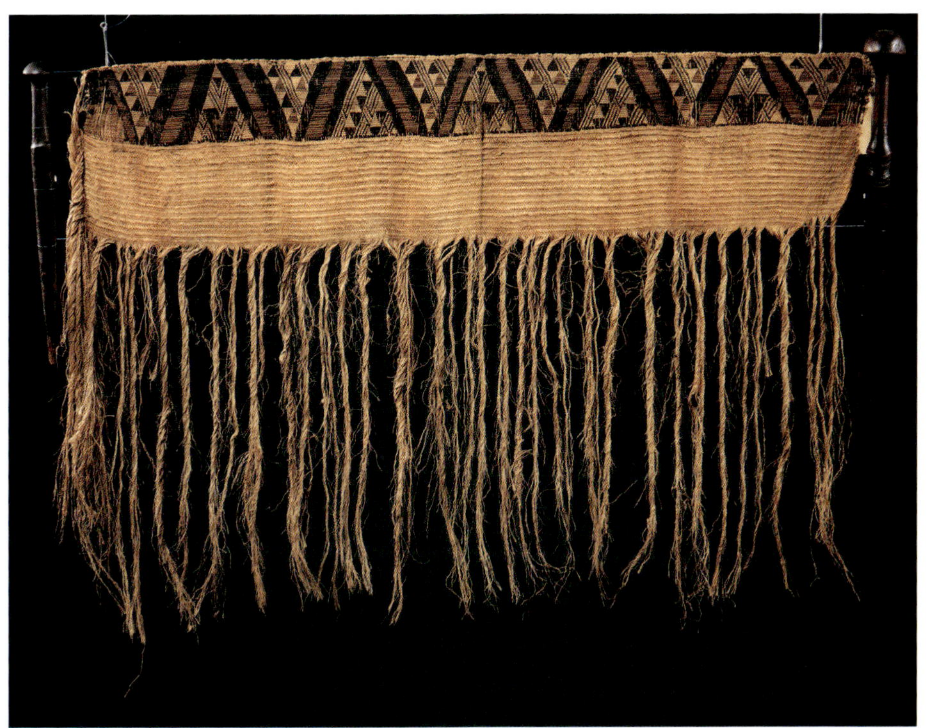

8B. unfinished kaitaka (cloak)
with a taniko border (AM 1079) strung between
turuturu whatu (left AM 1980, right AM 21894.2)
Auckland Museum Tamaki Paenga Hira
kaitaka presented by Mrs W. Raeburn in 1927;
left turuturu purchased Mr C. Spencer in 1928;
right turuturu from Sir George Grey collection no. 202

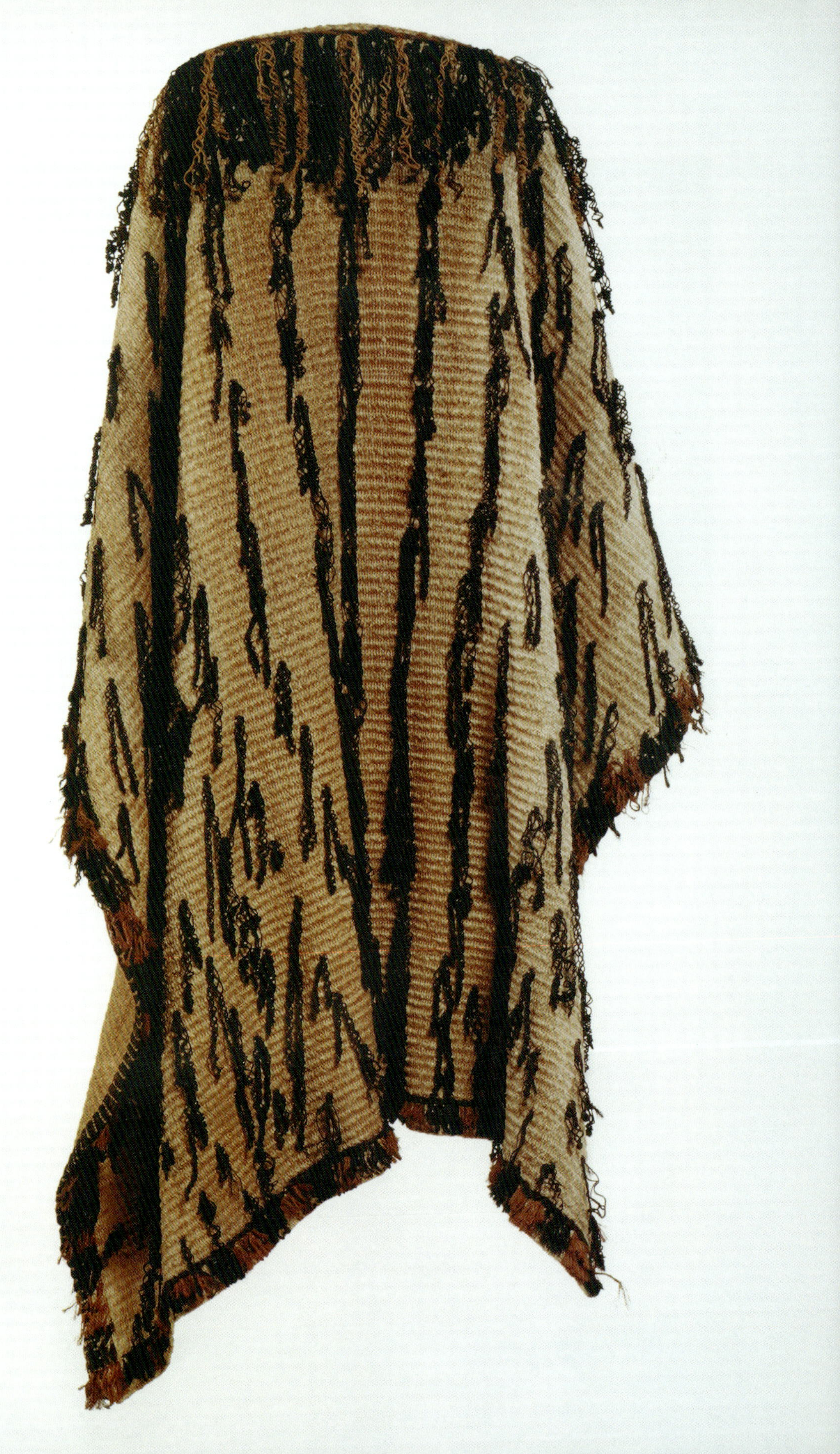

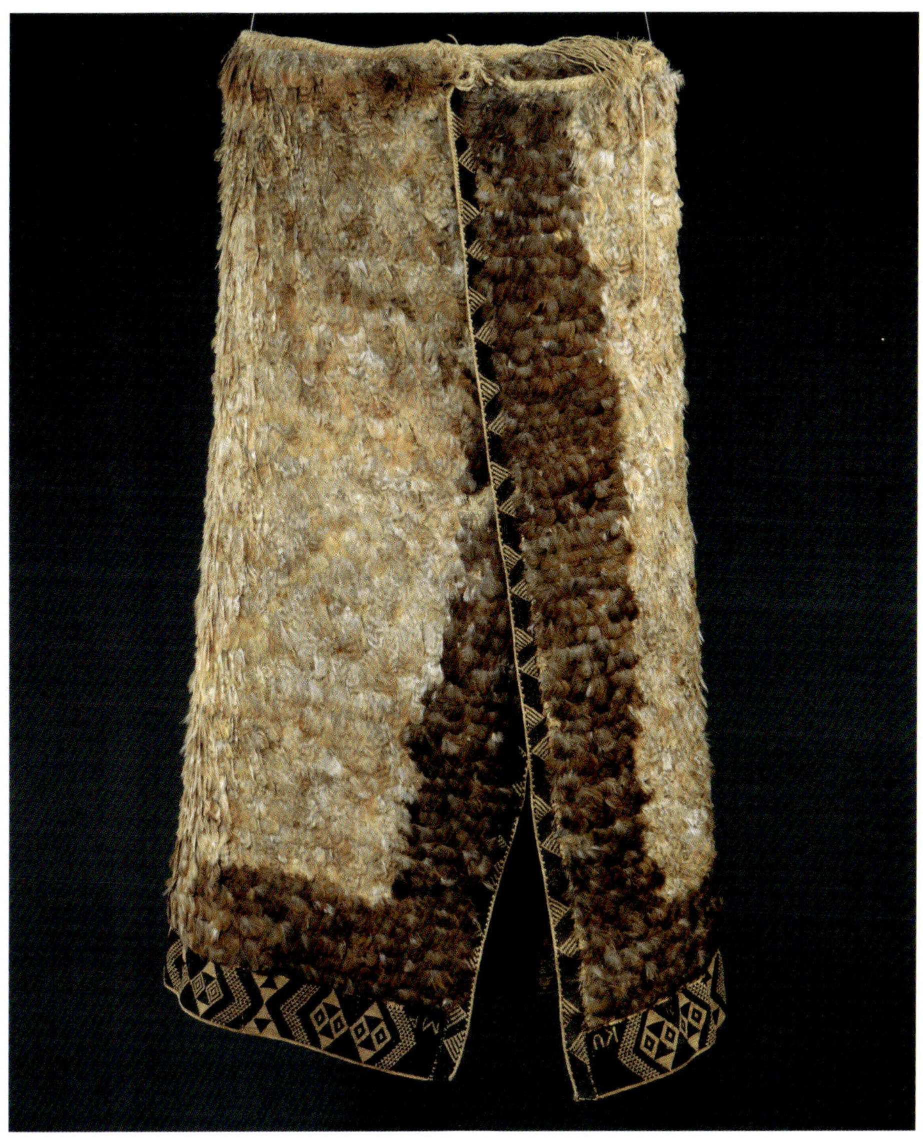

< 8C. korowai (cloak)
1230 mm (l) x 1460 mm (w)
flax fibre
Auckland Museum Tamaki Paenga Hira
AM 21677
photograph: Museum of New Zealand Te
Papa Tongarewa, Wellington O.027638

^ 8D. kahu huruhuru (feather cloak) with taniko
border
1050 mm (l) x 1360 mm (w)
flax fibre, kaka feathers
made by Makurata Paitini of Ruatahuna, c. 1900
Auckland Museum Tamaki Paenga Hira AM 5975
photograph: Museum of New Zealand Te Papa
Tongarewa, Wellington B.072682

9. RAUKATAURI

Raukatauri, or Raukataura as she is sometimes known in the north, is the goddess associated with flute music. Her original flute is the cocoon-like home of the female case moth, in which she now dwells, her calls audible as forest sounds. Maori wooden flutes, such as the straight koauau, curved nguru (pl. 9A) and long putorino (pl. 9B), are made in the form of the cocooned goddess, and playing them returns Raukatauri's voice to the world.

The first use of a musical instrument was to entertain. Raukatauri and her sister Raukatamea became part of an incognito female expedition sent to avenge the murder of their brother's whale by Kae, who had twisted his teeth in the process of consuming the creature. Flute music, as well as dancing and singing, were taught to villagers by the party to make them laugh until, finally, Kae was unmasked as the perpetrator, betrayed by his crooked smile. The story also explains the name of the 'taratara-a-Kae' notched pattern, used as a surface decoration on pataka carvings (pl. 9C). Apart from entertainment, flutes were used to mark events and attract attention, especially that of lovers. In the story of the couple Tutanekai and Hinemoa, the koauau and putorino music that he played on Mokoia Island was heard across Lake Rotorua and inspired Hinemoa to swim to him (pl. 9D).

The nguru can be played with the mouth or the nose, using the fingerholes to vary pitch. The interior of this small instrument is carefully hollowed out after the body has been shaped, but one of the most remarkable characteristics of some older nguru, apart from their distinctive weeping sound, is the profusion of intertwining decorations that adorn their surfaces (pl. 9A). These patterns are usually figurative, and their often highly abstracted forms are only identifiable by the irises looking out from a tangle of banded designs.

A putorino can be played as a flute or a trumpet through its end, or just as a flute into the middle 'mangai' (mouth) with one end covered. A versatile instrument, the sounds produced through blowing can range from a gentle high-pitched whistle to a deep bellow, or a haunting megaphonic resonance when the player sings into the chamber. The putorino's body is often adorned around its apertures with figurative decoration, interpreted by some as portraits of Raukatauri and associated beings. The rest of the body — a very thin cocoon — varies in surface decoration (pl. 9B). After shaping the instrument, a carver will split the body longitudinally to hollow out the core, reuniting and binding both sides when the process is complete.

As the voice of Raukatauri, Maori musical instruments are also devices to communicate with the ancestors and gods. With the Maori adoption of Christianity in the early to mid nineteenth century, such devices were no longer deemed appropriate, and the arts of instrument-making and playing almost disappeared until the late twentieth century. The recent revival has occurred, through examining museum-held examples and collecting oral narratives, under the leadership of Richard Nunns, Brian Flintoff and the late Hirini Melbourne.

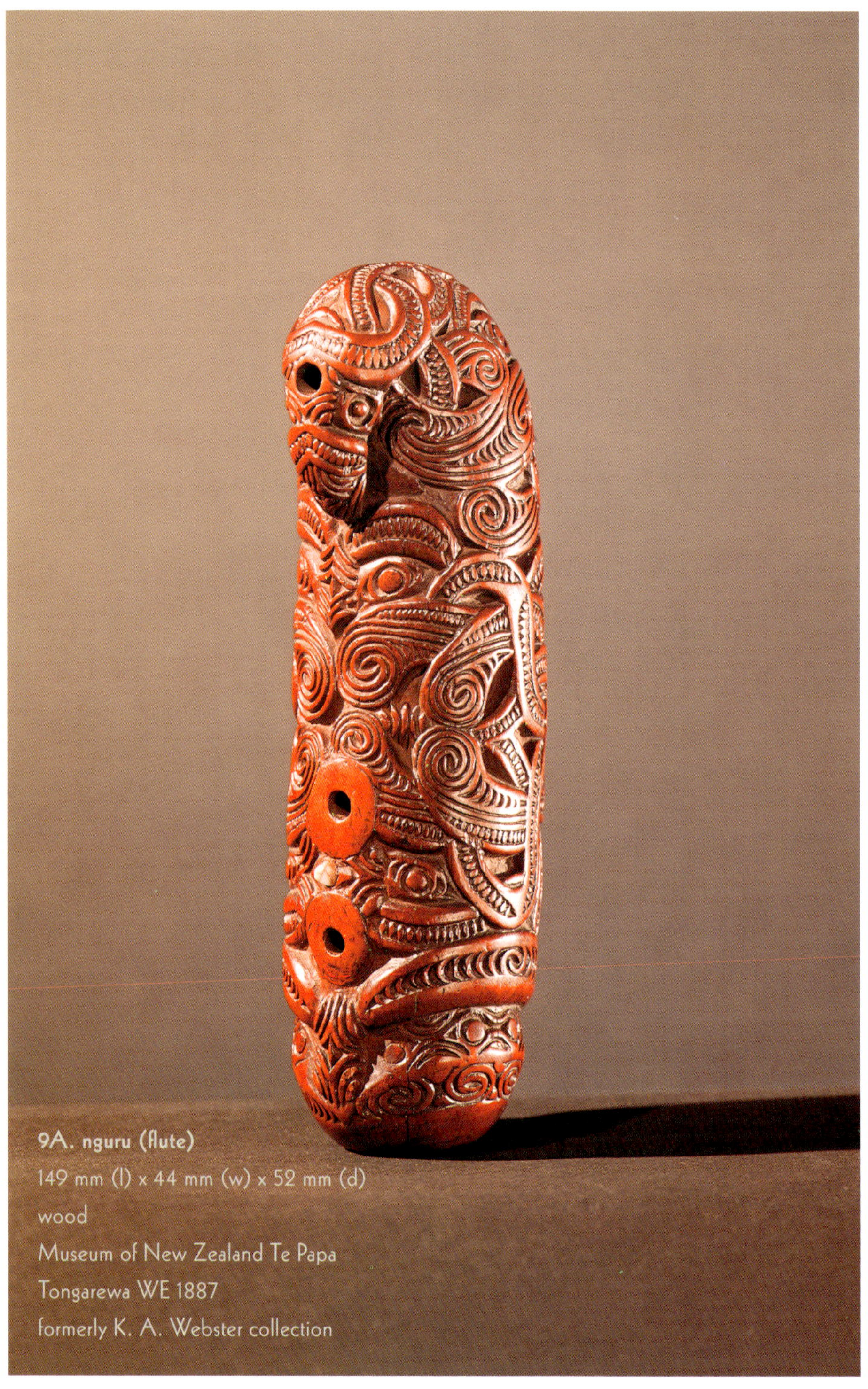

9A. nguru (flute)
149 mm (l) x 44 mm (w) x 52 mm (d)
wood
Museum of New Zealand Te Papa
Tongarewa WE 1887
formerly K. A. Webster collection

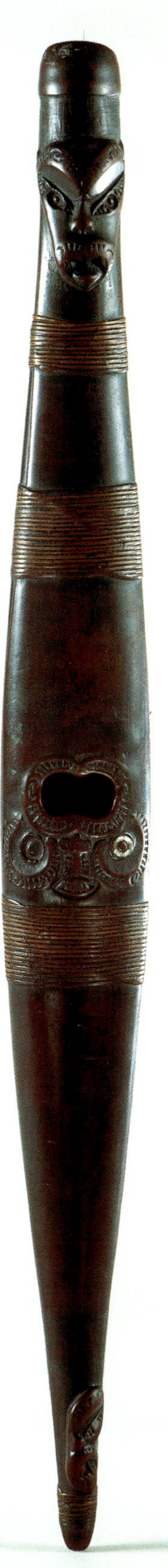

9B. putorino (flute or trumpet)
360 mm
wood, flax fibre
Auckland Museum Tamaki Paenga
Hira AM 36721
formerly K. A. Webster collection

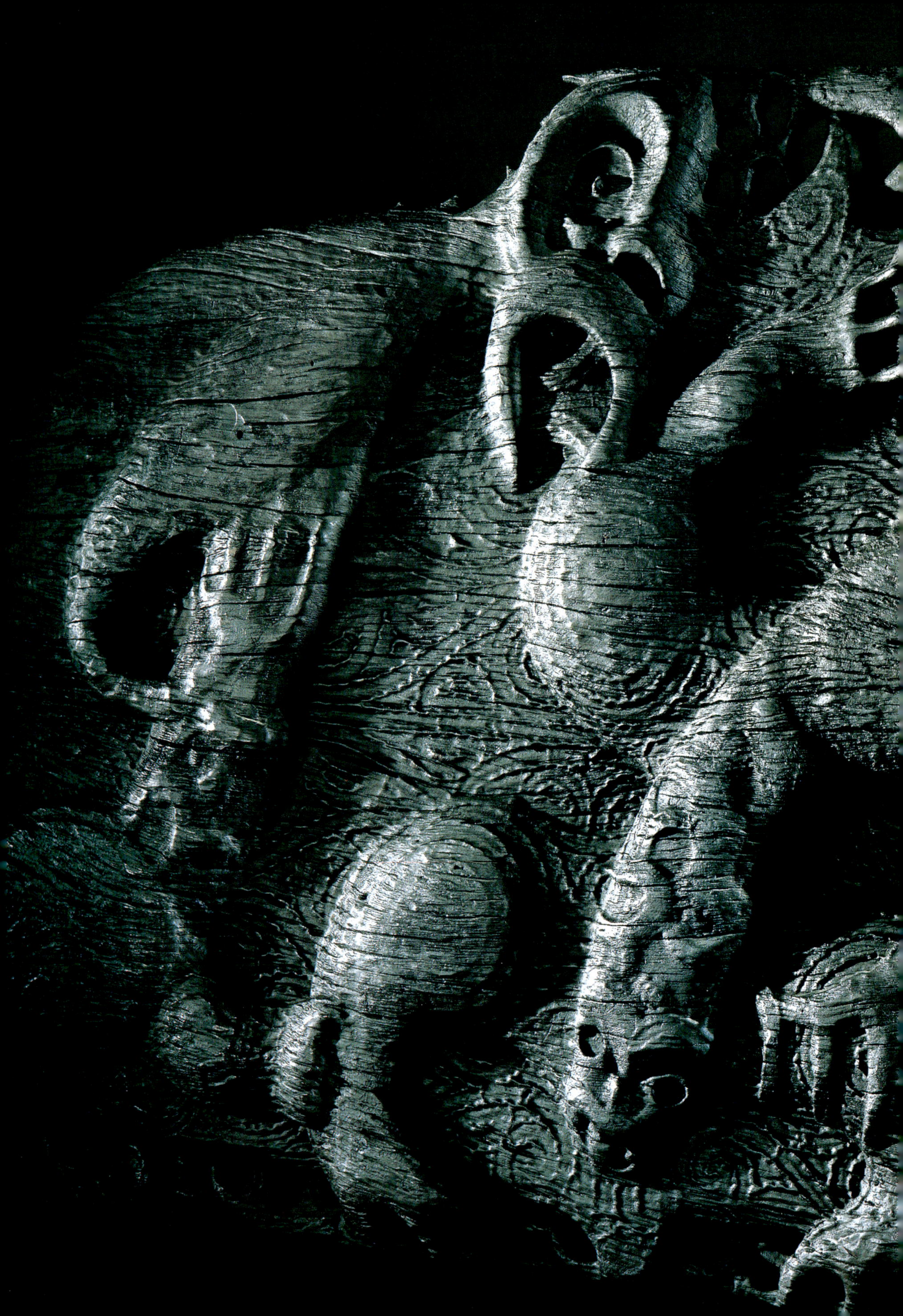

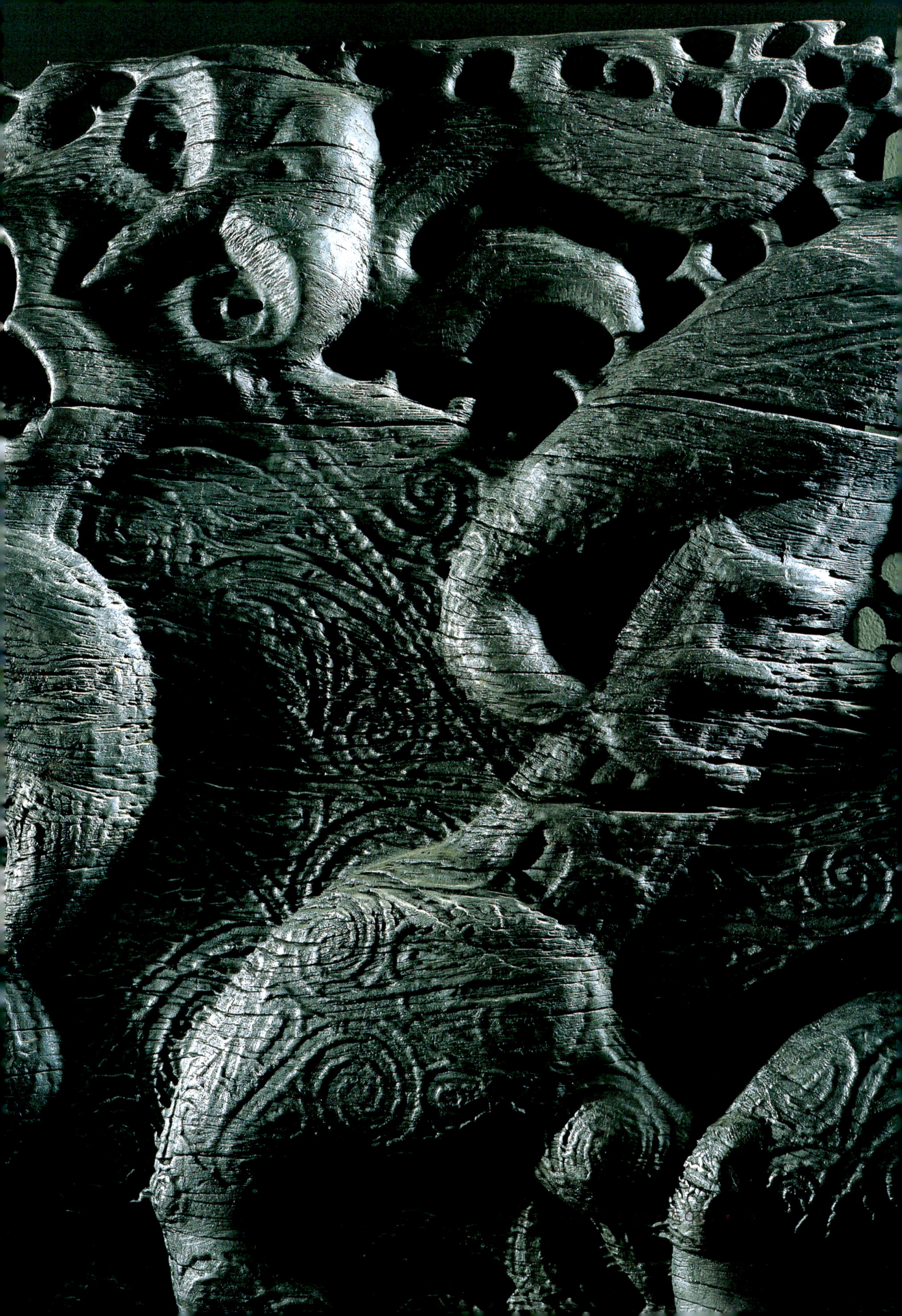

**« 9C. maihi (bargeboard) from Te Potaka pataka
(storehouse)**
totara wood
carved in the early nineteenth century
Auckland Museum Tamaki Paenga Hira AM 22063
formerly Spencer collection

**› 9D. kuwaha (gateway) depicting the
couple Hinemoa and Tutanekai**
wood
Whakarewarewa
carved by Tene Waitere in 1909

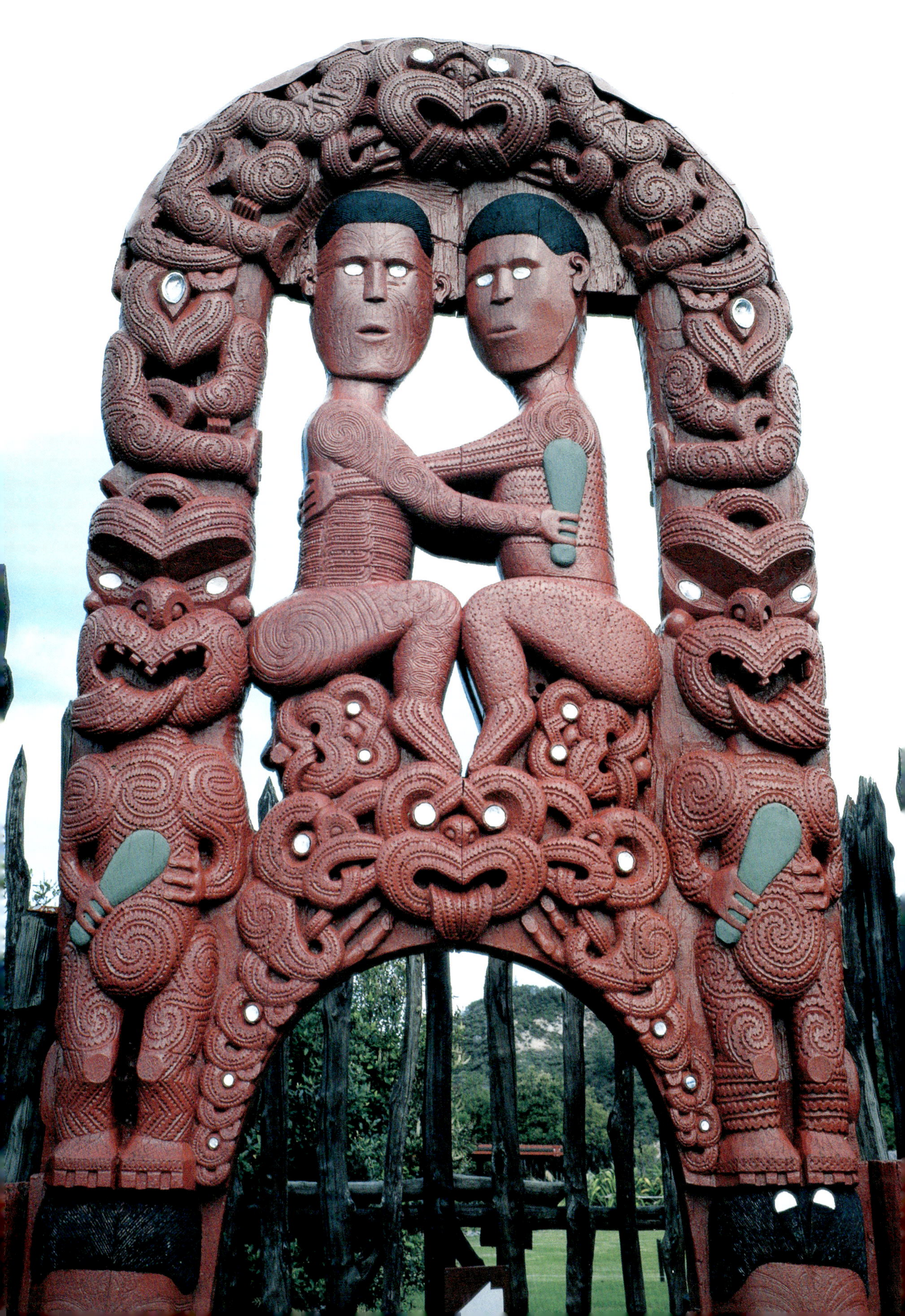

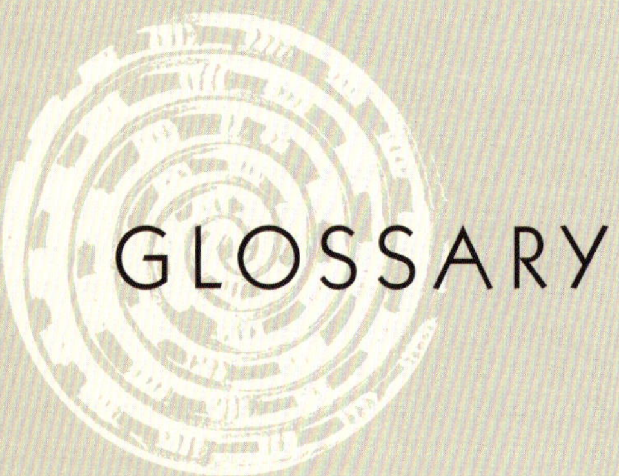

GLOSSARY

aho	weft	ko	digging stick
amo	front side panel of a building	koauau	straight flute
		kokowai	red ochre
		korere	feeding funnel
hahu(nga)	burial custom involving the cleaning and containment of human bones	korowai	cloak with fibre tag, and sometimes woollen, attachments
hapu	subtribe	koruru	front house gable apex mask
harakeke	flax, *Phormium tenax*		
haumi	canoe bow cover	kotiate	double-lobed cleaver
Hawaiki	ancestral homeland	kowhaiwhai	scroll painting
hei matau	fishhook pendant	kumara	sweet potato, *Ipomoea batatas*
heke	rafter		
Hineahuone	woman crafted from the earth by Tane	kuwaha	door, gateway
Hinenuitepo	goddess of death	maihi	bargeboard
Hinetitama	first human woman	mana	prestige, status
hue	gourd, *Lagenaria vulgaris*	mangai	mouth
ipu wai ngarahu	pigment pot	marae	tribal forum
ira tangata	human life force	marakihau	humanoid / fish hybrid carving character
iwi	tribe		
		Mataora	god associated with tattooing
kahu huruhuru	feather cloak		
kaikorero	orator	matau	fishhook
kaitaka	unadorned Maori cloak, often bordered with geometric taniko twining	Mauitikitikiataranga	legendary ancestor (also known as Mauipotiki)
		mauri	life force
karakia	incantations	mere pounamu	greenstone cleaver
kaupapa	cloak foundation garment	moko	Maori tattoo

moko kanohi — male facial tattoo
muka — harakeke sinews used in twining
nguru — curved flute
Niwareka — goddess associated with fibre arts
noa — free from tapu

pa — fortified village
Pakeha — New Zealand European
pane — porch ridgepole
papahou — rectangular treasure box
Papatuanuku — primeval mother, earth mother
pare — door lintel
pataka — raised storehouse
patu onewa — stone teardrop-shaped cleaver
patu paraoa — whalebone teardrop-shaped cleaver
poito — fishing float
pounamu — greenstone, New Zealand jade
pou — post, panel
poupou — wall post
poutokomanawa — freestanding house column
putorino — long flute or trumpet

rangatira — chief
Ranginui — primeval father, sky father
raranga — plaiting
Rarohenga — the underworld
rauawa — gunnels
Raukatauri — goddess of music (also known as Raukataura)
rei niho — whaletooth necklace
rei puta — eel-eyed whale tooth necklace
Ringatu Church — a Maori / Christian religion founded in the late nineteeenth century
Rongomatane — the god of cultivated foods

taha — gourd, calabash
tahuhu — ridgepole
taiaha — staff
ta moko — Maori tattooing process
Tane — the god of the forest
Tangaroa — the god of the sea

taniko — geometric cloak border pattern
taniwha — sea monster
taonga — treasure
tapu — restricted, sacred, special
taro — root, *Colocasia esculenta*
tauihu — prow
taurapa — stern
Te Ao — the white light, the world
Te Po — the black dark
tekoteko — front house gable apex figure
tiheru — bailer
tohunga — expert
tohunga whakairo — master carver
toki — adze
toki poutangata — ceremonial adze
tukutuku — lattice wall panel
Tumatauenga — the god of war
turuturu whatu — garment peg

utu — revenge, reciprocity

wahaika — cleaver
wairua — everlasting spirit
waka — vessel
waka huia — treasure boxes
waka taua — war canoe
waka tupapaku — bone casket (also known as waka koiwi)
whaikorero — formal oratory
whakairo rakau — wood carving
whakapakoko — 'god stick' used in divination rites
whakapapa — genealogy
whakawae — door jamb
whanau — extended family
whare — house
whare whakairo — decorated meeting house
wharenui — meeting house
whatu — fine twining
whenu — warp
whero — red

SELECT BIBLIOGRAPHY

Brake, B., *Maori Art: The photography of Brian Brake*. Reed Publishing, Auckland, 2003.

Brown, D., *Tai Tokerau Whakairo Rākau: Northland Māori wood carving*. Reed Publishing, Auckland, 2003.

Calman, R., revisions in A. W. Reed, *Reed Book of Māori Mythology*. Reed Publishing, Auckland, 2004.

Davidson, J., *Prehistory of New Zealand*. Longman Paul, Auckland, 1987.

Day, K., *Māori Wood Carving of the Taranaki Region*. Reed Publishing, Auckland, 2001.

Evans, J., *Maori Weapons in Pre-European New Zealand*. Reed Publishing, Auckland, 2002.

Flintoff, B., *Taonga Puoro: Singing treasures*. Craig Potton Publishing, Nelson, 2004.

Fox, A., *Carved Burial Chests: A commentary and a catalogue*. Auckland Institute and Museum Bulletin, 13, 1983.

King, M., *Moko: Maori tattooing in the 20th Century*. David Bateman, Auckland, 1992.

McLean, M., *Maori Music*. Auckland University Press, Auckland, 1996.

Mead, H. (S.), *Te Toi Whakairo: The art of Maori carving*. Reed Publishing, Auckland, first published 1986, reprinted 1995.

Melbourne, H. & R. Nunns, *Te Hekenga-a-Rangi*. DVD & CD, Rattle Records, 2003.

Neich, R., *Painted Histories: Early Maori figurative painting*. Auckland University Press, Auckland, 1993.

------ 'Wood Carving'. In D. C. Starzecka, ed., *Maori Art and Culture*. Bateman, Auckland, 1996: 69–113.

------ *Carved Histories: Rotorua Ngati Tarawhai woodcarving.* Auckland University Press, 2001.

------ & F. Pereira, *Pacific Jewellery and Adornment*, David Bateman, Auckland, 2004.

Oldman, W. O., *Oldman Collection of Maori Artifacts.* New edition of Memoir 14, Polynesian Society, Auckland, 2004.

Orbell, M., *Hawaiki: A new approach to Maori tradition.* Canterbury University Press, Christchurch, 1991.

------ *Illustrated Encyclopedia of Maori Myth and Legend.* Canterbury University Press, Christchurch, 1995.

Pendergrast, M., *Te Aho Tapu: The sacred thread.* Reed, Auckland, 2005.

Phillipps, W. J., *Maori Houses and Food Stores*, Dominion Museum, Wellington, 1952.

Prickett, N., *Nga Tohu Tawhito: Early Maori ornaments.* David Bateman, Auckland, 1999.

Tapsell, P., *Pukaki: A comet returns.* Reed Publishing, Auckland, 2000.

Te Awekotuku, N., 'Maori: people and culture'. In D. C. Starzecka, ed., Maori Art and Culture. Bateman, Auckland, 1996: 26–49.

------ *Ta Moko: Maori tattoo.* In R. Blackley, ed., *Goldie*, David Bateman & Auckland Art Gallery, Auckland, 1997: 109–114.